WHY CAN'T THEY BE LIKE US?

Also by Andrew M. Greeley

RELIGION AND CAREER:
A Study of College Graduates

THE EDUCATION OF CATHOLIC AMERICANS
(with Peter H. Rossi)

WHAT DO WE BELIEVE?
(with Martin E. Marty and Stuart E. Rosenberg)

RELIGION IN THE YEAR TWO THOUSAND

WHY CAN'T THEY BE LIKE US?

America's White Ethnic Groups

By Andrew M. Greeley

E. P. Dutton & Co., Inc. | New York | 1971

Published simultaneously in Canada by
Clarke, Irwin & Company Limited, Toronto and Vancouver

Library of Congress Catalog Card Number: 72-148473

SBN: 0-525-23370-9

Grateful acknowledgment is given to the American Jewish Committee for
permission to reprint herein substantial portions of *Why Can't They Be Like
Us?* by Andrew M. Greeley, Copyright © 1969 the American Jewish Committee.

Chapter 10, "Intellectuals as an Ethnic Group," first appeared in *The New York
Times Magazine*.

For Pat Moynihan—the last of the old ethnics
or maybe the first of the new ones:
May the ancient saints of Erin
—Patrick, Brigid, Columkille and all the rest
—continue to smile upon him.

Acknowledgments

This book began originally with a paper presented at a consultation sponsored by the American Jewish Committee. I am very grateful to Irving M. Levine and Judith Herman of the AJC for their constant encouragement.

My thinking on ethnic groups has been notably influenced by the most subtle Florentine since Niccolo Machiavelli—Peter H. Rossi—to whom my debt for ethnicity (though not for everything else I owe him) is hereby noted. Daniel P. Moynihan has consistently encouraged my interest in ethnicity and by both word and being persuaded me that ethnicity still lives. Norman M. Bradburn, the director of the National Opinion Research Center, who is not an ethnic (but says he feels like one whenever I am around), has facilitated my interest in the subject, and my colleague, Galen Gockel, who definitely is an ethnic, provided me with some fascinating tabulations. Nella Seifert typed the first manuscript with her usual persistent care. Virginia Quinn, who is an ethnic but not of the sort her name indicates, suffered with patience through typing the present form of the book. Nancy McCready, than whom no one I know is more ethnic, has been an appropriate ethnic research assistant.

Contents

"It is often said this city is a melting pot. That is not true. It is rather a series of small towns and neighborhoods. The strength of our city is in the addition of many separate cultures and traditions.

"The most stable of all our neighborhoods in New York City are those neighborhoods that have preserved traditions of language, traditions of dress, traditions of style, of food, of look. Every person in our city came from somewhere."

—John V. Lindsay

WHY CAN'T THEY BE LIKE US?

Introduction

This is a book about diversity in American society, not about all the different kinds of diversity, but specifically about the diversity caused by the immigration of white ethnic groups from Europe to America between 1820 and 1920. The religious and ethnic pluralism caused by this migration is not the most important sort of diversity in American society. It certainly does not threaten to tear American society apart; but because it is not the most important, it is not thereby unimportant. Quite the contrary, ethnic pluralism is part of the very fabric of American urban life (especially in the North Central and Northeast regions of the country). American social science has ignored this diversity for more than a quarter of a century and American policy makers ignored it in formulating the social policies of the 1960's. To some extent, the failure of those policies derives from the abysmal ignorance of both social scientists and social policy makers about the subject of ethnic pluralism. Recently, they have rediscovered the subject although the perspectives from which they insist on viewing it may well make matters worse instead of better.

If I have a basic theme in this book, it is that he who wishes to accomplish social change in the large American urban centers must know something about the ethnic pluralism of these centers. He cannot be content with the arrogance of those who write off all white ethnics as "racist" or "fascist" or, to use a word fashionable at the time I write this introduction, "hard hats." Even if the experience of white ethnic groups sheds no light at all on the problems of more recent immigrants to the large cities (and I think it does shed some light), nevertheless, all who wish to fight poverty and injustice in the city must firmly understand that in a democratic society you cannot accomplish social change without some sort of broad consensus in favor of that change. During the turbulent 1960's it was thought that some shortcuts for the creation of political consensus were possible. "Protest," "violence," even "revolution" were advocated as the means by which a minority could impose its will on the majority (one social scientist even argued that it was necessary to abolish majority rule in order to accomplish social change; the alternative, of course, to majority rule is minority rule and we once had a real revolution in this country on that subject). In fact, however, since 1967 most "direct action" efforts, peaceful or violent, have been counterproductive while, on the contrary, the election of black mayors in several American cities with the help of white voters has established that a broad political consensus is not by any means impossible.

This volume is not intended as a handbook for political action, but as a preliminary effort at understanding. Even if it were not necessary to achieve political consensus of some sort in American cities during the 1970's, the subject of white ethnic groups would still be fascinating and indeed indispensable for understanding American society.[1]

Some Americans become very uneasy when the subject of religious and ethnic diversity is raised. They insist that even to speak about the subject may be wrong since it emphasizes what is different among us instead of what is the same. It is all right for the blacks and the Chicanos and the American Indians to have some sort of ethnic consciousness, but for other American groups ethnic consciousness is, somehow or other, immoral. This unease is manifested, I find, particularly among those who have just left their own ethnic heritage behind, convinced that it represents a benighted past and that they must shed their ethnic identity to become truly a part of American society. I suspect that such people have a feeling of guilt about what has been left behind and a feeling of fear that it has not been left behind completely. Rejection of their own ethnic identity has become for them a matter of principle. They react vigorously and moralistically to the suggestion that American society is wrong to demand rejection of ethnic identification, for all that such a demand probably is self-defeating. Professor Michael Parenti, in

The American Political Science Review, summarizes the case for the persistence of ethnic identification in American society:

We can see that (a) increases in education have not necessarily led to a diminished ethnic consciousness; indeed, the increase in sectarian education often brings a heightened ethnic consciousness. (b) Increases in income and adaptation to middle class styles have not noticeably diminished the viability and frequency of ethnic formal and informal structural associations. Such stylistic changes as have occurred may just as easily evolve *within* the confines of the ethnically stratified social systems, thereby leading to a proliferation of parallel structures rather than absorption into Anglo-Protestant social systems. (c) Geographical dispersion, like occupational and class mobility, has been greatly overestimated. Movement from the first settlement area actually may represent a transplanting of the ethnic community to suburbia. Furthermore, as we have seen, even without the usual *geographic* contiguity, *social* and *psychologically* contiguous ethnic communities persist. (d) Intergroup contacts, such as may occur, do not necessarily lead to a lessened ethnic awareness; they may serve to activate a new and positive appreciation of personal ethnic identity. Or intergroup contacts may often be abrasive and therefore conducive to ethnic defensiveness and compensatory in-group militance.[2]

I do not of course wish to argue with those men and women who have rejected their own ethnic heritage, yet do not find themselves fully accepted in the larger society. In their marginal situation they cannot be expected to be dispassionate on the subject. This volume, nonetheless, takes as its basic assumption a fact that is obvious to anyone who ventures beyond the university confines of our large cities: Ethnic diversity is alive and well.

But I should like to make an even stronger case for the importance of ethnic diversity and the mere fact that, like the Rocky Mountains and the Mississippi River, it is there. Claude Lévi-Strauss, the French anthropologist, in his study of totems, points out that within a given tribe totemic symbols represent different creatures but always creatures of the same class. Thus, in an Indian tribe, the totemic clans may be the bears, the lions and the rams and in another tribe the hawks, the eagles and the falcons, but in no tribe (save the National Football League) will the falcon clan and the bear clan coexist. In other words, according to Lévi-Strauss, the totemic clans function to diversify the tribe as a prelude to structural integration. They create tribal unity, not through homogenization of membership, but rather through a diversification which is perceived as a prelude to integration. Diversity, in Lévi-Strauss' view of things, is essential for human society because it is diversification that creates social structure. In primitive totemic clans the symbols of diversification point toward integration. That which is different is not completely different. Quite the contrary, it is perceived as different in such a way as to work toward unity.

Unity does not, of course, follow automatically. In the human condition, diversity easily becomes a basis for distrust, suspicion and conflict. We find it profoundly disturbing that others are different from us; indeed, the very title of this book is the battle cry of the ethnic screaming for homogenization of society, but an homogenized society would not exist for very long because it would have no social structure. The critical problem then for those who wish to expand the area of trust and love in human relationships is not to eliminate diversity but to understand how diversity can be integrated in some form of unity. The differences between male and female, white and nonwhite, young and old, better educated and less educated are perennially the focus of social conflict, nor does it seem likely that such tensions can be eliminated. The critical question is how to use these tensions and diversities to create a richer, fuller human society instead of a narrow, frightened and suspicious society.

The emergence of a multi-ethnic society in the United States in a relatively brief period of time is one of the most astonishing social phenomena of the modern world. That such a society should be torn by conflict is not surprising; what is surprising is that it exists at all. I would not be so foolish as to claim that all the answers to the strains and tensions that come from human diversity can be found in the study of American ethnic groups but I think it not at all unreasonable to suggest that the study of ethnic diversity in the United States can be extremely helpful in understanding the fundamental problem of human diversity. This book is based on extensive social research. Unfortunately, for reasons I note later, very little research has been done on American ethnic groups. While this volume will have some of the statistical data which is so dear to social scientists, and particularly to survey researchers like myself, the data will at best be sketchy. The book is merely a preliminary investigation, and hopefully more careful and detailed research will be done in the years ahead. If the readers of this book, particularly the young readers, are motivated to collect data which disprove many of my assertions, I will not merely rejoice but I will also (and this is a singular admission from a social scientist) cheerfully admit that I am mistaken. Should the volume be fortunate enough to go into a later edition, I'll even correct the mistakes, hoping that I don't lose my union card for such an unorthodox practice.

One final point must be made. Some of the more militant black spokesmen, and some of their more guilt-ridden white allies decry the study of white ethnic diversity on the grounds that it is an attempt to turn away from the legitimate demands of blacks. No other social problem, these spokesmen tell us, ought to be considered until something is done about the injustices that have been visited upon American blacks. Interest in ethnic groups, we are told, is a form of white racism.

I categorically reject the charge. I am not a white racist and he who accuses me of being one is in fact a racist himself. I do not for a moment question the prior claims blacks have for justice in American society but I will assert that the blanket charge of white racism, in addition to being racist itself, is politically and socially counterproductive. Furthermore, I contend not merely that the study of white ethnic diversity will facilitate justice for American blacks but, in the absence of greater understanding of urban diversity, this justice is likely to be delayed even longer.

Some of the new interest in ethnic groups may, indeed, be an attempt to head off black progress. Some of it may be a reaction to heightened black self-consciousness. But I sense a rather different relationship between black ethnic consciousness and the new "awareness" among white ethnic groups of their own identifications. What the blacks have done is to legitimate ethnic self-consciousness. The Poles, the Italians, the Slovaks, the Hungarians, even the Germans and the Irish, have always been more or less conscious of their own heritage and identification, but it was not considered good form in the larger society to talk about such subjects, save on approved days of the year like Columbus Day or St. Patrick's Day. Now black nationalism has legitimated ethnic self-consciousness and white ethnics say with perfect reasonableness, "If they can be proud of their heritage every day in the year and explicitly proud of it, why can't we?" Why not, indeed?

Injustices were done to many of the ethnic groups when they came to America. The ancestors of present elite groups who are so concerned about the injustices being done to today's poor were anything but concerned about the injustices done to turn-of-the-century immigrants. Nor have the American elites completely abandoned their prejudice against the children of these immigrants. The Yale professor whom Michael Lerner quotes [3] as suggesting that the Italians are an inferior people (because Mario Procaccino dared to run against John Lindsay) and the stereotypes of Italian gangsters on the mass media would indicate that there are still those who wonder "why the Italians can't be like us."

And the Polish jokes, and even worse, the stereotype of Stanley Kowalski which the mass media and even such would-be elite magazines as Harper's seek to perpetuate in discussing Polish ethnic groups, would suggest that American Poles have not yet received a fair break from the host society (the picture of a large, half-naked "hard hat" draped over a bar in a Harper's article on Gary, Indiana, gives some indication of the image of the Pole that still lurks in the collective semiconscious of those who illustrate magazine articles).

Furthermore, while magazines (such as Harper's in the nineteenth century) no longer print cartoons in which Paddy is displayed as a gorilla with a club in one hand and a pint of beer in the other, one wonders if anti-Irish feeling has been completely purged. Such diverse Irish politicians as Richard Daley and Daniel Patrick Moynihan might well be viewed differently by the intellectual elite if they were not Irish.

I am obviously not arguing that discrimination against the Irish or the Italians or the Poles is or was anything like that which our black brothers have had to endure, but I am suggesting that bigotry is by no means a lower-class phenomenon and that compassion among the elites is by no means universal. And yet, an attitude of compassion towards one group mixed with bigotry towards another group is, in the final analysis, intolerable—intolerable on moral grounds because it is hypocritical and intolerable on political grounds because it is self-defeating. The intellectual who "loves" the blacks and the "poor" but has contempt for the Irish or the Italians or the "middle class" is in the final analysis every bit as much a bigot as the blue-collar worker who "hates niggers," for both are asking, "Why Can't They Be Like Us?" And to this titular question in this book there can be but one satisfactory answer: "Because they don't want to be and in the United States of America, they don't have to be."

Notes

1. By political consensus I mean only the barest minimum; that is to say, the absence of opposition powerful enough to frustrate social change. For an example of how such a minimum consensus was needlessly and foolishly destroyed in one city read the introduction to the second edition of *Beyond the Melting Pot* by Nathan Glazer and Daniel Patrick Moynihan (Cambridge: MIT University Press, 1970).

2. Michael Parenti, "Ethnic Politics and the Persistence of Ethnic Identification," *American Political Science Review* (September 1967).

3. Michael Lerner, "Respectable Bigotry," *American Scholar* (August, 1969).

Chapter 1.
A Nation of Immigrants

When this manuscript was first begun, teachers in New York City were involved in the third strike of the academic year, and the school children of New York City had had two months of extra vacation which they may have welcomed, but about which their parents and the political leaders in the city and the state were anything but enthusiastic. The causes of that strike were many and complex, and all are not really pertinent to this volume, but one way of looking at the conflict is to see it as a struggle between trade unionists, mostly but not entirely Jewish, determined to defend the traditional rights of union members won through many hard decades of strikes and collective bargaining, and black militant leaders and followers, determined to have control over what is taught in the schools their children attend and who teaches in these schools. While the press may have softened somewhat the ethnic nature of this conflict, one had only to watch the brief television interviews with either side to realize that most of the names and the faces and the accents on one side were Jewish and on the other side black.

The schools are now open, but the issue is far from settled. Two American ethnic groups previously thought to be allied were suddenly involved in fierce combat; at issue was power and, unfortunately, the amount of power available is limited or presumed to be limited. If the blacks are to have the power they want over decentralized school systems, then the United Federation of Teachers with its heavy component of Jewish membership is, in all likelihood, going to lose power.

The blacks want more control over their local affairs, and the only way they will get more control, many of them feel, is to take it away from the dominant ethnic group in the situation—an ethnic group which happens to be Jewish. Thus, American

Jews, easily the most liberal and progressive ethnic group in the country, find themselves faced with the possibility of battle with another ethnic group toward whom they have traditionally felt very sympathetic, and on whose side they have been in many other controversies.

I cite the New York City teachers' strike for a number of quite different reasons:

First of all, even though the blacks and the Jews are more than ethnic groups, the former being a racial group and the other a religious group, their conflict is cut from the mold of a typical American interethnic conflict. An older, more established and more powerful immigrant group is faced with the demands for increased power from a new, militant and very determined immigrant group. These conflicts are part of the history of American society, and particularly of American cities, and if the truth be told, show no signs of ending.

Thus, the example of the New York teachers' strike as an ethnic conflict will indicate how the term "ethnic group" will be used in these pages. For all practical purposes, we can equate ethnic group with immigrant group—though I hope to clarify the terms somewhat as I go along. Since even the American Indians were immigrant groups to this continent, we are quite clearly, as President Kennedy said, a nation of immigrants; and many, if not most, of the group conflicts that occur in the United States can be interpreted as a struggle between immigrant groups for what they think is their fair share of power in the society. These immigrant groups may also be racial or religious groups, and the racial and religious overtones of the conflicts make them even more serious; but it seems to me that the basic social dynamic at the root of ethnic conflicts is the struggle of immigrant groups for political and social power.

Secondly, the New York conflict ought to indicate, if proof were necessary, that there is no pair of ethnic groups which cannot, given the proper circumstances, lock horns with each other. It would have been inconceivable to many people a decade ago that there could be ethnic conflict between Jews and blacks. When Norman Podhoretz, the editor of *Commentary*, wrote an article a few years back bravely exploring the possibility of anti-Negro prejudice among Jews, the outraged reaction of many Jewish readers showed how unthinkable such conflict was considered. Yet the raw material of such a confrontation was already present, for there were two very large immigrant groups coexisting in the same geographical location, one possessing a great deal of socioeconomic and political power and the other possessing very little. The astute observer—and Podhoretz was certainly one—would have suspected that, should the weaker group seek to improve its position, conflict was almost inevitable.

My third point in citing the New York teachers' strike is that the political leadership and the social planners who determined on school decentralization seem to have been completely unaware of the hornets' nest they were stirring up. Yet anyone who had spent much time studying American ethnic groups would have been quite capable of warning political leaders and the social planners that they might be getting into very deep trouble, and that it would be wise to prepare for it. And, as a matter of fact, a number of trained behavioral scientists did sound such warnings; but they were obviously not taken seriously.

It is no criticism of Mayor Lindsay's administration to say that a Democratic leadership might have been a little less likely to make the same mistake, for the Democratic party, founded as it is in the art of balancing ethnic communities one against another, has always had to be more aware of the realities of ethnic communities than has the Republican party. Indeed, the secret of Irish control of many American cities is that they are the most adept at playing the role of broker among other ethnic groups.[1]

One suspects that when the social historians of, let us say, the twenty-third or twenty-fourth century look back on the era that we now presume to describe as the modern world, they will find two or three social phenomena of extraordinary interest. One, certainly, is the demographic revolution—the astonishing increase in the population level of the world that has occurred in the past century and a half. The second will be the westernization and industrialization of the non-Western world. And the third, unless I miss my guess, will be the formation of a new na-

tion on the North American continent made up of wildly different nationality groups. The historians of the future will find it
hard to believe it could have happened that English, Scotch and
Welsh, Irish, Germans, Italians and Poles, Africans, Indians,
both Eastern and Western, Frenchmen, Spaniards, Finns,
Swedes, Lebanese, Danes, Armenians, Croatians, Slovenians,
Greeks and Luxembourgers, Chinese, Japanese, Filipinos and
Puerto Ricans would come together to form a nation that not
only would survive, but, all things considered, survive reasonably well. I further suspect that the historians of the future will
be astonished that American sociologists, the product of this
gathering in of the nations, could stand in the midst of such an
astonishing social phenomenon and take it so much for granted
that they would not bother to study it.

They will find it especially astonishing in light of the fact that
ethnic differences, even in the second half of the twentieth century, proved far more important than differences in philosophy
or economic system. Men who would not die for a premise or a
dogma or a division of labor would more or less cheerfully die
for a difference rooted in ethnic origins. Chinese and Malay
fight each other in Southeast Asia; Ibo and Hausa in Nigeria;
Greek and Turk on Cyprus; Czech and Slovak in Czechoslovakia; Arab and Jew in the Middle East; black (at least so-called)
fights white (at least relatively) in the United States;[2] and the
French and the English, running out of colonial peoples with
which to contend, now renew the feud that the Hundred Years'
War never did settle. Finally, along the lines of the Shamrock
curtain, another feud simmers, and Frank O'Connor's immortal
words, spoken from the secure position of his own agnosticism,
are as true as ever: "The north of Ireland contains the best Protestants in the world and the south of Ireland the best Catholics,
and there is nary a single Christian in the whole lot."

Immigration, Acculturation, Assimilation

Fashions in thinking, both popular and scholarly, about ethnic
groups have changed. It was first assumed that the cultural
forces of American society, particularly as applied in the public

school system, would rather shortly level the differences among American immigrant groups and that most of the immigrants would, in effect, become good white Anglo-Saxon Protestants, speaking what Professor Peter H. Rossi[3] once labeled "radio-standard English." Even though the naïve "melting pot" notion has long since lost its scholarly respectability, it is still, one suspects, a latent but powerful influence in American society. As members of older immigrant groups say of members of younger immigrant groups, "Why don't they act like us?"

More recently, the idea of "cultural pluralism" emerged, which saw the United States not only as a nation of immigrants, but as a nation of immigrant groups; the immigrants, it was explained, would become American and thoroughly American, but at the same time retain much that was distinctive and creative about their own cultural heritage, perhaps even including their own language. A good deal of romantic prose has been written about how one nation is formed out of many, and about how Poles, Armenians, Italians, Jews, Irish, Hungarians and any other ethnic group one cares to mention can retain their own traditions and still be thoroughly and completely American.

Somewhere between the melting pot and cultural pluralism is the notion of the "multiple melting pot," first advanced by Ruby Jo Reeves Kennedy[4] and made popular by Will Herberg.[5] In this view the old immigrant groups were collapsing, but three superethnic groups based on religion were replacing them. One would, therefore, no longer think of oneself as German or Swedish or Irish or Romanian, but rather as Protestant, Catholic or Jew.

A more sophisticated social science approach has been developed recently under the influence of S. N. Eisenstadt[6] and Milton Gordon,[7] who hypothesize two kinds of assimilation: cultural assimilation or acculturation, which involves the process of the immigrant group learning the manners and the style of a new society, and structural assimilation (or simply assimilation) in which the members of the immigrant group relate to members of other groups, particularly on the intimate levels of friendship and family formation, without any regard to ethnic differences. Eisenstadt and Gordon suggest that acculturation is taking place among immigrant groups, but not assimilation. Irish, Polish, Jews, blacks, Armenians, Romanians, Greeks and so on, dress in the same kind of clothes, read the same magazines, watch the same television shows, perform the same kinds of jobs, share the same kinds of political and social values, but still, to a very considerable extent, seek their intimate friends and their marriage partners from within their own ethnic group. According to this theory, acculturation can go on at a relatively rapid rate, and even create a certain pressure for assimilation without making assimilation anywhere near complete, and therefore ethnic groups continue to survive and probably will do so for the foreseeable future. This assimilation-acculturation view seems to combine the best perspective of both the melting pot and the cultural pluralism approaches, but this does not necessarily mean that it is the best possible explanation for what's going on.

Another suggestion is found, however implicitly, in the excellent books written by Daniel Patrick Moynihan and Nathan Glazer [8] and Herbert Gans.[9] These writers tend to view ethnic groups as essentially interest groups, which came into being because of common origin and cultural background and continue in existence as the most appropriate units through which their members can seek greater political, social and economic power for themselves. Their assumption is that cultural differences among ethnic groups are declining rapidly, if they have not already been eliminated, and that it is the common interest in political and socioeconomic power which keeps the groups together.

There is nowhere near enough empirical data to make any confident assertions about the validity of the various approaches described above. Nevertheless, my colleague Peter Rossi and I are inclined to view the last two described with some reservation. We do not want to deny that the ethnic communities are very powerful interest groups; nor that acculturation seems to be going on at a faster rate than assimilation. But we are still forced to wonder why common national origin would be the basis for organizing and sustaining an interest group, and we would also wonder whether even acculturation has gone on quite as rapidly as some observers might think. To say, for example, that blacks and Swedes and Armenians share the same values is to speak a truism, at least up to a point; but anyone who has dealt with the three groups is well aware that in addition to the commonality of values, there is great diversity across these three groups—a diversity which may not be so great as to tear the fabric of American society apart, but is great enough to make them different kinds of communities.

In other words, we are not ready to assume that vast cultural differences do not persist. Our suspicion—and given the present state of the data, it is little more than suspicion—is that the core of these differences has to do with different expectations about close relatives; that is, in one ethnic group the expectations of how a husband or a wife, a father or a mother, a brother or a sister, a cousin, an aunt, or an uncle should behave are likely to be quite different than in another ethnic group. There is enough legend about Jewish mothers and Irish mothers for us to be able to realize that the expectations of these two ethnic groups, while in some sense quite similar, are also very, very different. But if we throw into the discussion the somewhat less known expectations of how a Missouri Synod German Lutheran mother ought to behave, we become quite conscious of how complex the question of the survival of ethnic differences really is.

The question is made even more complex by the fact that the various immigrant groups came here at different times, both in the development of the society they left behind and in the development of American society.[10]

European Origins and American Experience

As Nathan Glazer has pointed out, the Germans came from a society that was a nation long before it had become a state, and many of the German immigrants saw no reason why they could not create a German nation in the midst of the American continent (and as part of the American Republic). The Irish were not so inclined to create an Irish nation, although on one occasion they did attempt to invade Canada to take it away from England. But both these groups came quite conscious of their nationality, and quite capable of setting up ethnic enclaves, whether in rural Iowa or urban Boston (the Germans chose the country far more than did the Irish), that were based on the concept of nationality.

The second type of immigrant group, according to Glazer, was the Scandinavians who indeed came from states, but states that were not yet nations; for the Scandinavian peasants saw themselves less as members of nations than citizens of villages or members of a religious community. The Norwegians and the Swedes came to think of themselves as Norwegians and Swedes only when they banded together here to form communities of their fellows, particularly in the rural areas where the Scandinavians tended to settle. Glazer observed that it was easier for the Swedes and Norwegians, who had less of a notion of nationality than the Irish, to create nationality enclaves, because the Irish were in the city and the Swedes and Norwegians were in the country. In Glazer's words,[11] "We can, I think, conclude that where these early immigrants were isolated and remained rural, they showed an amazing persistence in maintaining the old language, religion, and culture. . . . For those . . . in the cities . . . a shorter time sufficed to remove the language and culture they had brought with them."

Glazer observes that among more recent immigrants, there are large numbers of people who came from nations struggling to become states (Poles, Lithuanians, Slovaks, Croatians, Slovenians), or from states struggling to become nations (Italy and Turkey and Greece), as well as from areas outside these Western concepts (Syrians), and of course one group—the Jews—who fit appropriately into none of these state-nation categories. "The newcomers became nations in America," Glazer points out quite succinctly; and he quotes with approval the insight of publisher Max Ascoli, "They became Americans before they ever were Italians."

In two remarkable paragraphs, Glazer describes the astonishing phenomenon of the emergence of European "nations" in the American environment.

> . . . Indeed, the effort of creating a national language, a task which the Western European nations had accomplished centuries

before, was considerably facilitated for these Eastern peoples by American emigration. The coming together in American cities of people of various villages speaking various dialects required the creation of a common language, understood by all. The first newspaper in the Lithuanian language was published in this country, not in Lithuania. The urbanization of many East European peoples occurred in America, not in Europe, and the effects of urbanization, its breaking down of local variation, its creation of some common denominator of nationality, its replacement of the subideological feelings of villagers with a variety of modern ideologies—these effects, all significant in making the East European peoples nations, were in large measure first displayed among them here in America. The Erse revival began in Boston, and the nation of Czechoslovakia was launched at a meeting in Pittsburgh. And all this should not surprise us too much when we realize that some European areas were so depopulated that the numbers of immigrants and their descendants in America sometimes equaled or surpassed those who were left behind.

If nations like Czechoslovakia were in large measure created here in America, other immigrants were to discover in coming to America that they had left nations behind—nations in which they had had no part at home. Thus, the American relatives of Southern Italians (to whom, as Ignazio Silone and Carlo Levi describe them, the Ethiopian war meant nothing more than another affliction visited upon them by the alien government of the North) became Italian patriots in America, supporting here the war to which they would have been indifferent at home.[12]

We do not have nearly as much historical information as we might about the early phases of the immigrant experience. Nevertheless, a vast amount of data was collected by the so-called Dillingham Commission in its study of immigrants in the United States at the beginning of the century. It would be a mistake to treat the immigration commission data as if it were comparable with the far more sophisticated data that we have at our disposal at the present time. But, despite the fact that the Dillingham Commission was primarily concerned with justifying more restrictive immigration policies, its several shelves of reports still contain a gold mine of information about the status of ethnic immigrant groups shortly after the turn of the century.

That some of the children of immigrants were able to make more rapid progress in American schools in 1910 than others is evident from Table 1. As one might expect, the children of the immigrant Irish-born parents did as well in moving through the public school system as did native born whites since they were not at a language disadvantage, but Germans, both Christian and "Hebrew" (the word is the Commission's, not mine), are only somewhat more likely to be "retarded" than are the members of English-speaking groups. Furthermore, there is a difference of more than twenty percentage points between the children of the Northern Italian immigrants and Southern Italian immigrants, with Russian "Hebrews" being closer to the Northern Italians, and Polish immigrants being closer to the Southern Italians in their retardation rates.

Obviously, more is involved than simply language or even nation of origin. The cultural and social environment from

TABLE 1
RETARDATION RATES AMONG CHILDREN
IN PUBLIC SCHOOLS IN THIRTY AMERICAN CITIES
IN 1910 BY ETHNICITY AND GENERATION

	Percent retarded*
Native-born	
White	28
Negro	67
Indian	48
Foreign-born	
English	27
Irish	29
German	32
Hebrew German	32
Hebrew Russian	42
Italian Northern	42
Italian Southern	63
Polish	58

* Two years or more older than normal for their grade.
SOURCE: Adapted from Table 15, page 31, *Reports of The Immigration Commission: The Children of Immigrants in Schools.* Vol. 1, (Washington: U. S. Government Printing Office, 1911).

which the immigrants came as well as the selective reaction to the immigrants by the host society are factors that are unquestionably important. Furthermore, the state of organization of the immigrant community into which the most recent immigrants moved must also have been a factor at work. Despite many volumes on the social history of immigrant groups, however, the most that can be said about the data reported in Table 1 is that we have some clues toward an explanation—but the clues come dangerously close to stereotypes.

The various immigrant groups also experienced differential economic success in the United States in 1910. Native-born Irish (second generation) made on the average $204 more a year than native-born Southern Italians, while foreign-born Irish (first gen-

TABLE 2
ANNUAL INCOME OF MALES 18 YEARS AND OLDER
BY ETHNICITY AND GENERATION

	Income*
Native-born of native parents	
White	$666
Negro	445
Native-born of foreign-born parents	
English	586
Irish	612
Italian — Northern	402
— Southern	408
Polish	537
German	619
Hebrew	492
Foreign-born	
English	673
Irish	636
Italian — Northern	480
— Southern	396
Polish	428
German	579
Hebrew	513

* SOURCE: Adapted from Table 54, page 407, *Reports of the Immigration Commission: Abstracts of the Reports of the Immigration Commission.* Vol 1, (Washington: U. S. Government Printing Office, 1911).

eration) made $240 a year more than foreign-born Southern Italians. On the other hand, the income difference between the Irish and the Polish in the first generation was $208 a year and in the second generation only $75 a year.

Nonetheless, the basic findings of Table 1 persist in Table 2. The Irish do moderately well in income in both generations, most likely because of their knowledge of English, but the Germans, who do not know English, are substantially more successful in both generations than the Polish or Italians. It is also worth noting that the annual income of both first and second generation Southern Italians was less than that of American Negroes in 1910.

In Table 3 we note that even within a given industry—the iron and steel industry—income differentials persist. Italian and Polish immigrants and their children were considerably less well off than the Germans, Irish and English.

TABLE 3
WEEKLY EARNINGS IN THE IRON AND STEEL INDUSTRY
IN 1910 BY ETHNICITY AND GENERATION

	Weekly earnings[*]
Native	
White	$16.54
Negro	10.64
Native-born of foreign parents	
English	17.26
German	16.43
Irish	16.00
Italian	11.43
Polish	—
Foreign-born	
English	18.56
German	14.38
Irish	15.83
Italian — Northern	11.80
— Southern	10.59
Polish	12.09

[*] *Ibid.* Adapted from Table 38, p. 384.

Unfortunately, sophisticated methodology was not available in 1910 and we cannot guarantee that the educational background was the same for any given type of job within the iron and steel industry that members of the different immigrant groups held. However, even if we reject the implied racism that ran through much of the immigration commission's findings at the turn of the century, not much doubt exists that some immigrant groups were much more successful in escaping from poverty conditions than others.

The three factors of immigration and the acculturation process mentioned previously (the social and cultural conditions from which they emigrated, the reception by the host society and the organization and sophistication of the immigrant community) explain a good part of the differences. Thus, Southern Italians came from a relatively disorganized, peasant society, were viewed with grave dismay by their American hosts (even to the extent of establishing a separate category for them in the Dillingham reports) and in 1910 immigrated into an ethnic community which was only beginning to be organized. The Irish, on the other hand, came with language and political skills and immigrated into a well organized ethnic community, strongly reinforced by the Roman Catholic Church and, if not exactly welcomed by the host society, at least were able to force the host society to respect their political power.

However, it is difficult to create anything more than a very tentative link between such historical statements about the differential immigration experience of various ethnic groups and the figures in Tables 1 to 3. At best, one is reduced to a statement of cautious hypothesis which, given the state of sociological study, may never be more than an hypothesis. Nevertheless, one assertion can be made with considerable confidence—that membership in an ethnic group puts members of that group at a relative advantage or disadvantage in their efforts to go up the stratification pyramid and to leave poverty behind them.

We will turn later to the question of whether the ethnic groups whose history we have so briefly summarized will continue to survive in American society. Glazer is inclined to think that in the long run they will not, but that will be a very long run. My own inclination would be to think, rather, the opposite. America's ethnic groups are rooted only very partially in the European preimmigrant experience, and have been shaped to a very great extent, however differentially for different groups, by the American experience. Glazer is quite right in saying that the Italo-Americans are very different from the Italo-Italians, and I can testify from personal experience that while the Irish-Irish and the American-Irish are in some respects similar, they are also very different. But this does not mean that American-Irish are about to become indistinguishable from American-Italians.

The ethnic group in this perspective is a combination of European cultural background, American acculturation experience (different for different groups), and political, social and economic common interest. Not merely do different origins produce cultural differences; the different experiences in America reinforce the old differences and create new ones. The Kennedy administration was, one supposes, quite different from the administration of Prime Minister Sean Lynch in Dublin, but it was also very different from a WASP administration in this country, or the kind of administration we will have when finally Americans get around to electing a Jewish president.

There are a number of reasons why intensive study of American ethnic groups is long overdue. First of all, as we pointed out earlier, the wandering of the nations which has produced the United States of America is one of the most extraordinary social phenomena in the whole history of mankind. It provides us with a marvelous laboratory for the study of human relationships. What is there, precisely, in presumed common origin that attracts us to others of similar origin and repels us from those of different origins? Ethnic interaction and conflict in American society can tell us many things about human relationships that we are only beginning to dimly understand.

Secondly, our society faces immediate social problems which cannot be solved unless we understand more about the operation of the ethnic factor. I need not look at the statistics to be summarized later in these pages about Polish attitudes on racial questions to know that there is an acute problem in the relationship between Poles and blacks—at least one need not look at statistical tables if one lives in Chicago. Nor, if one lives in New York City, is it possible any longer to be unaware of the tension between Jews and blacks. If we understood more about how ethnic groups relate with one another, we might have some insights which would enable us to mitigate, if not eliminate, the dangerous tensions which threaten to tear apart our large cities.

Finally, it might be easier to understand the problems of the new immigrant groups if we were somewhat more aware of how older immigrant groups coped with their problems at a similar state in the acculturation process. I certainly do not want to subscribe to any interpretation of American racial problems which says that the blacks are just like any other ethnic immigrant group, and that their problems will be solved in the same way as the problems of the Irish or the Slovaks or the Italians or the Jews. For however degrading were the life conditions of the early white immigrants, they were at least not brought here as slaves nor kept in slavery or near-slavery for several hundred years. Nor are their skins a different color from that of other Americans. The combination of the slavery-serfdom experience and the difference in skin color (which, whether we liberals like it or not, still seems to be a universal human problem) puts the blacks at a much more serious disadvantage in acculturating to American society and obtaining their full rights than any previous group.

Nevertheless, there are certain similarities in the process through which all immigrant groups must pass in American society, and if we keep in mind that these are similarities and not exact identities, we can find them very illuminating. For example, there is, to my knowledge, not a single accusation that has been made by whites against American blacks that was not previously made against my Irish ancestors, with the possible exception that while blacks are accused of a high addiction to narcotics, the Irish were accused of an undue consumption of John Barleycorn. It was said of both groups that they were shiftless, irresponsible, pleasure-loving, violent, incapable of learning American ways, culturally inferior, too emotional religiously and immoral (as proven by the high crime rates in their districts). The only basic difference that I can determine is that when the

Irish rioted, they really did so in a big way. Nothing the blacks have yet done compares with—let us say—the antidraft riots of 1863 in New York. Similarly, when the Irish engaged in guerrilla warfare, they were far more ruthless and effective; the blacks have not yet, thank God, tried to match the Molly McGuires.[13]

Finally, one may also study ethnic groups simply because they are interesting, and because, of all the branches of social science, the study of ethnic groups generates more amusing stories (that are not pejorative to anyone) than any other branch of the discipline. Presumably American society needs all the humor it can get at the present time; within American society there is no segment more in need of laughter than the social sciences. But I wouldn't count on much laughter being tolerated there yet.

Notes

1. It is unfashionable to say anything kind about Chicago's Mayor Daley, at least east of the Indiana border, but it is still worth noting that in the last Chicago election Daley was able to obtain the majority support of both the black and the Polish communities in Chicago, a political feat of rare skill. Given the stresses of the times, it is dubious whether Chicago would be at all governable unless its leadership were able to attain consensus from both of these groups. There may be other ways of obtaining such consensus than the Daley political style, but there is little evidence that his opposition possesses such skill.

2. An earlier and somewhat shorter version of this material appeared in the international journal, *Concilium*, Vol. 4, No. 3, April 1967.

3. Professor Peter H. Rossi was for many years Director of the National Opinion Research Center at the University of Chicago, and is now Chairman of the Sociology Department at Johns Hopkins University.

4. Ruby Jo Reeves Kennedy, "Single or Triple Melting Pot? Intermarriage Trends in New Haven," *American Journal of Sociology*, 49 (January 1944), pp. 331–39.

5. Will Herberg, *Protestant-Catholic-Jew* (New York: Doubleday, 1955).

6. S. N. Eisenstadt, *Essays on Comparative Social Change* (New York: Wiley, 1965).

7. Milton Gordon, *Assimilation in American Life* (New York: Oxford University Press, 1964).

8. Daniel Patrick Moynihan and Nathan Glazer, *Beyond the Melting Pot: The Negroes, Puerto Ricans, Jews, Italians and Irish of New York City* (Cambridge: Harvard and MIT University Press, 1963).

9. Herbert Gans, *The Urban Villagers* (Glencoe, Ill.: The Free Press, 1962).

10. In this section I lean heavily on an article by Nathan Glazer: "Ethnic Groups in America," which is part of the symposium, *Freedom and Control in Modern Society*, by Monroe Berger, Theodore Abel and Charles H. Page (New York: Van Nostrand, 1954).

11. Nathan Glazer, *op. cit.*, p. 165.

12. Nathan Glazer, *op. cit.*, pp. 166–67.

13. The best way to assure oneself a steady stream of hate mail is to make these assertions to an audience that contains a fair number of the sons of St. Patrick. Usually the letters begin with, "And you a priest!" and conclude with references to how generous the Irish were to the Catholic Church, or with obscene references to the presumed sexual immorality of blacks. Generally, too, the writers will include some remark about how the Irish had to work for what they got, while the blacks are unwilling to work. My own presumption is that both Irish and blacks, like any other ethnic group, have similar proportions of compulsive workers and compulsive loafers. Anyone who thinks that all the Irish earned their living is unaware of the masterful skill of Irish political leaders in days gone by in keeping the shiftless and indolent alive through the use of political payrolls. And in certain cities, these activities have not yet ceased.

Chapter 2.
What Is an Ethnic?

It is very difficult to speak precisely about what an ethnic group is, but it is possible to develop a working definition somewhat empirically and to describe ethnicity by showing how contemporary ethnic groups came into existence. While, as I indicated earlier, there is some broad equation possible between ethnic groups and immigrant groups, it is not enough merely to say that the ethnic groups are immigrant groups. Whatever definition we emerge with is likely to leave us with some very embarrassing questions. For example: Does everyone belong to an ethnic group? Is a white Anglo-Saxon Protestant an ethnic? Are Texans or Kentuckians, for example, ethnics? And what about American intellectuals, particularly those who are not Jewish and who seem to be quite cut off from any trace of nationality background? Do they constitute a new ethnic group (see Chapter 10)? Such questions do not admit of quick answers; yet we must address ourselves to them if only because there are a number of Americans who are not prepared to take ethnic issues seriously unless responses to those questions are provided.

The ancestors of the immigrants to the United States were, for the most part, peasants living in the agricultural communities of European post-feudal society. This society was post-feudal in the sense that the peasants either owned some land of their own, or at least had been emancipated from the worst rigors of the feudal system. The peasant villages of Ireland, Germany, Italy, Poland or the Balkans were not the most comfortable places in the world, and the nostalgia bordering on romance over them that is to be found in the works of some nineteenth century sociological writers is misleading. Granted that post-feudal peasant society provided a great deal of stability, it did so at the price of stagnancy; and granted also that it provided a great deal of social support, it did so by imposing a great deal of social control. A man was, indeed, sure of who he was and where he stood and what he might become in such societies, but most men were in inferior positions and had no expectation of becoming anything more than inferior.

Nevertheless, there was a warmth and intimacy and closeness in these peasant communities. A person could be sure of the pattern of relationships and be sure that while he might have enemies, he also had friends, and the friends and enemies were defined by historic tradition. Society indeed controlled individual members, but it also rallied support, strength and resources when help was needed. It was a highly personal world, not in the sense that the dignity of the human person was respected more than it is today, but in the sense that relationships were, for the most part, between persons who knew each other, understood their respective roles and knew what kind of behavior to expect. Family, church and community were all fairly simple and overwhelmingly important, and though mankind had evolved beyond the all-pervading intimacy of the tribe or the clan, life was nonetheless quite personal and intimate in a stylized and highly structured way.

Some time after 1800, European peasant society began to break up, partly because, as the population increased, there were more people than jobs in the agricultural communes, and partly because the emergent industrialization in the cities desperately needed new labor. Those who made the move from commune to metropolis in hope of finding a better life began a number of social trends which actually meant a better life, if not for them, at least for their children or their grandchildren. The pilgrimage from peasant village to city, and later to the cities of America, brought to many the wealth of the affluent society.

But something was also lost: the warmth and intimacy, the social support of the commune was gone. Gabriel Le Bras, the famous French sociologist of religion, remarked that there was a certain railroad station in Paris which apparently had magical powers, because any Breton immigrant who passed through that station never set foot in a Catholic church again. The church, the family, the commune which had provided the parameters of the ordinary person's life were all either destroyed or so substantially altered as to be unrecognizable. The peasant migrant was forced to spend most of his waking day with people who were strangers. This is an experience which does not seem peculiar to us at all, but to a man who had encountered few strangers ever before in his life, it was frightening and disorienting.

"Our Own Kind"

In the strangeness of the new environment, the individual or his battered and bedraggled family looked around for someone with whom he had something in common—hopefully a place in the big city where previous migrants from his village had settled. Because such settlers were "his kind of people," he could trust them; they knew their obligations to him and would help him to adjust to this new world in which he found himself. Thus, in the Italian neighborhoods of New York's lower east side in the early 1920's it was possible to trace, block by block, not only the region in Italy but also the very villages from which the inhabitants had come. Indeed, it is no exaggeration to say that some of these blocks were nothing more than foreign colonies of Sicilian villages.

If you weren't able to find someone from your own village, then you searched for someone from your area of the country; even though you may never have met him before, you could depend on him to have some of the same values you had, and you shared some sort of common origin. He may not have been from Palermo, but at least he was a Sicilian; he may not have been from Ballyhaunis, but at least he was from County Mayo; and these village or regional groupings, based especially on family and kinship relationships, in their turn sought protection and some power against the strange world in which they found themselves by banding together, one with another. So that for many groups, as Glazer has pointed out, the nationality became a relevant factor only when the necessities of adjusting to American experience forced the village and regional groups to band together.

The ethnic group provided a pool of preferred associates for

the intimate areas of life. It was perhaps necessary in large corporate structures to interact with whomever the random possibilities of the economic system put at the next workbench or
desk. But when it came to choosing a wife, a poker (and later
on, bridge) partner, a precinct captain, a doctor, a lawyer, a
real estate broker, a construction contractor, a clergyman and,
later on, a psychiatrist, a person was likely to feel much more at
ease if he could choose "my kind of people."

So then, as Max Weber [1] defines it, an ethnic group is a
human collectivity based on an assumption of common origin,
real or imaginary; and E. K. Francis,[2] supplementing the Weber
definition, has argued that the ethnic collectivity represents an
attempt on the part of men to keep alive, in their pilgrimage
from peasant village to industrial metropolis, some of the diffuse, descriptive, particularistic modes of behavior that were
common in the past. The ethnic group was created only when
the peasant commune broke up, and was essentially an attempt
to keep some of the values, some of the informality, some of the
support, some of the intimacy of the communal life in the midst
of an impersonal, formalistic, rationalized, urban, industrial society.

That the immigrants tried to associate with their own kind
was understandable enough in the early phases of immigration,
but we are still faced with the necessity of explaining why ethnic groups have persisted as important collectivities long after
the immigration trauma receded into the background. Why was
not social class the membership around which American city
dwellers could rally, as it was in England? Why have the trade
unions rarely, if ever, played quite the fraternal role in American society that they have in many continental societies?
Granted that urban man needed something to provide him with
some sort of identification between his family and the impersonal metropolis, why did he stick with the ethnic group when
there were other groupings to which he could make a strong
emotional commitment?

First of all, one must acknowledge the fact that other groups
have, on occasion, provided the same enthusiasm that ethnic
groups do. Some men need more of this enthusiasm than others,

and by no means all who need it seek it in a nationality group. As a matter of fact, it is probably likely that for many, at least at the present stage of acculturation, religion is more important than ethnicity as a means of social definition and social support, a means of identifying ourselves in relation to others. However, religion and ethnicity are so intertwined in the United States that it is extremely difficult to separate them; an attempt to sort out this relationship is one of the major challenges facing social theorists who become concerned with ethnic groups.

Pluralism and Group Survival

It seems to me that there were two factors which made for the survival of ethnic communities after the immigration trauma was over. First of all, the United States is a society which has demonstrated considerable ability in coping with religious and racial pluralism, one way or another. A nation which was, in effect, religiously pluralistic before it became politically pluralistic, the United States had to learn a sufficient amount of tolerance for religious diversity merely to survive. It was necessary only to expand this tolerance when the new immigrant groups arrived on the scene with their own peculiar kinds of religious difference. It also seems that, even before the Revolutionary War, nationality differences were important, so the Germans and the Irish (usually meaning the Scotch-Irish) were considered as a group quite distinct from the Anglo-Saxon majority. Furthermore, even though the racial relationship had deteriorated into tyranny and slavery, there was, at least until the invention of the cotton gin, apparently some possibility that even this might be peacefully settled. In other words, by the time the large waves of immigrants came, in the early and middle nineteenth century, America was already acquiring some skills in coping with the religiously and ethnically pluralistic society. The immigrants were not welcome, and considerable pressure was put upon them to become Anglo-Saxons as quickly as possible. Yet the pressures stopped short of being absolute; the American ethos forced society to tolerate religious and ethnic diversity even if it did not particularly like it. Under such circumstances, it was possible for the ethnic groups to continue and to develop an ideology which said they could be Irish, German, Polish or Jewish, and at the same time be as good Americans as anyone else—if not better.

But why is it still important to be an Italian, an Irishman, a German or a Jew? Part of the reason, I suspect, has something to do with the intimate relationship between ethnicity and religion. But another element, or perhaps another aspect of the same element, is that presumed common origin as a norm for defining "we" against "they" seems to touch on something basic and primordial in the human psyche, and that, as we pointed out in the previous chapter, much of the conflict and strife that persists in the modern world is rooted in such differences. If anything, the separatist nationalisms within the major nation states seem stronger today than they were a quarter of a century ago: Catholics rioting in Londonderry, Ireland; Scots electing nationalist members to Parliament; the mutterings of Welsh separatism. The Basques, and even the Catalonians, grumble about being part of Spain; the Flemings and the Walloons are at odds with each other over Louvain; the Bretons wonder if it might be possible for them to escape from France; and the French Canadians are not at all sure they want to remain part of the Canadian nation, even if they could have their own prime minister.

Most of these separatist movements make little sense in terms of economic reality. The Province of Quebec would be hard put to go it on its own; Wales and Scotland would very quickly have to form a political and economic union with England, not much different from the one that already exists; and Brittany would have to do the same with the government in Paris. Maybe tribal loyalties and tribal separatism ought not to continue in a rational, industrial world—but they do, and it is a threat to the fabric of almost any society large enough to be made up of different ethnic communities. One is almost tempted to say that if there are no differences supposedly rooted in common origin by which people can distinguish themselves from others, they will create such differences. I suspect, for example, that if Scotland did become independent of England, there would be conflict between the Highlanders and the Lowlanders as to who would run the country. Ethnic diversity seems to be something that man grimly hangs on to, despite overwhelming evidence that he ought to give it up.

University of Chicago professor Edward Shils has called these ties primordial and suggests that, rooted as they are with a sense of "blood and land," they are the result of a prerational intuition. Such an assumption seems to make considerable sense, but is difficult to prove empirically. It is certainly true, however, that family, land and common cultural heritage have always been terribly important to human beings, and suspicion of anyone who is strange or different seems also to be deeply rooted in the human experience. Ethnic groups continue, in this hypothesis, because they are a manifestation of man's deep-seated inclination to seek out those in whose veins he thinks flows the same blood as flows in his own. When blood is also seen as something intimately related to belief, and both blood and belief impinge strongly on what happens to a man, his wife and his children, he is only too ready to fight to protect the purity of that belief, or the purity of his blood, or the purity of his family when it is threatened by some strange outside invader.

This view of ethnicity, it must be confessed, is essentially a negative one. But one can make a more positive case for it. It could be said that the apparent inclination of men, or at least of many men, to consort with those who, they assume, have the same origins they do, provides diversity in the larger society and also creates substructures within that society that meet many functions the larger society would be hard put to service. And while the demons of suspicion and distrust prove very hard to exorcise from interethnic relationships, such suspicion and distrust are not, I am convinced, inevitable. If they can be eliminated, ethnicity enriches the culture and reinforces the social structure.

To sum up, ethnic groups have emerged in this country because members of the various immigrant groups have tried to preserve something of the intimacy and familiarity of the peasant village during the transition into urban industrial living. These groups have persisted after the immigrant experience both because American society was not basically hostile to their persistence and because of an apparently very powerful drive in man toward associating with those who, he believes, possess the same blood and the same beliefs he does. The inclination toward such homogeneous groupings simultaneously enriches the culture, provides for diversity within the social structure and considerably increases the potential for conflict. It may some day be possible to isolate ethnicity from suspicion and distrust, but no one has yet figured out the formula for doing so.

Notes

1. Max Weber, "The Ethnic Group," in Talcott Parsons, et al. *Theories of Society*, Vol. 1, p. 305 (Glencoe, Ill.: The Free Press, 1961).

2. E. K. Francis, "The Nature of the Ethnic Group," *American Journal of Sociology*, 52 (1945), p. 393.

Chapter 3.
The Functions of Ethnicity

Before we turn to the role of ethnic groups in contemporary American society, we must face some of the insistent questions that were raised in the previous chapter.

First of all, is everyone an ethnic? In one sense, of course, the answer to such a question is an obvious yes. It is true that all our ancestors at one time did migrate to the American continent. But does national origin seem important to everyone? Here the response must be no. For some people ethnic background is very meaningful both because it affects their behavior and is an important part of their self-definition. For others, ethnic identification may be completely unimportant and ethnic background may have little influence on their behavior. In other words, ethnicity is one of a number of ways in which Americans may identify themselves and which they may use as part of their self-definition. At the social-psychological level, then, not everyone is an ethnic. But the relevant question seems to be—under what sets of circumstances do which people express what sort of ethnic identification? When is ethnicity relevant, and for whom? Unfortunately, American behavioral science cannot answer that question at the present time.

One suspects, however, that ethnicity becomes very important in three sets of circumstances: 1) When an ethnic group is very large and has great actual or potential political and economic power. It is probably far more meaningful to say that someone in Chicago is Polish than to say that Senator Muskie of Maine is Polish. And to be Irish probably means much more in Boston than it does in Tallahassee, Florida. 2) When one is a member of a small but highly visible or well-organized minority. To be Mexican or black is probably always important, because these background characteristics are almost always highly visible. 3)

When a sophisticated group suddenly becomes conscious that it has become a minority and is surrounded by many other well-organized ethnic communities. Thus, to be a white Anglo-Saxon Protestant in, let us say, Nebraska may not be nearly as meaningful as to be the same thing in New York City, when one suddenly discovers that one is, indeed, a member of a minority group—and a minority group which, for all its economic power and social prestige, enjoys (or at least enjoyed, until recently) very little in the way of political potential. Visibility, sudden recognition of minority status, or being a large group in an environment where ethnic affiliation is deemed important—these three variables may considerably enhance social-psychological and social-organizational influence of ethnic groups.

Perhaps the most critical issue that can be raised about ethnic groups is the nature of their relationship to religious groups. Will Herberg's answer was simple enough—the ethnic groups are dissolving into the superethnic community provided by one of three major American religious groupings. But it is apparent that Herberg was somewhat premature in his judgment. To be a Norwegian Protestant is by no means the same as to be a Southern Baptist; nor is it the same as to be a Missouri Synod Lutheran. Similarly, Irish Catholicism and Polish Catholicism are very different phenomena and provide very different kinds of identification. The mutual resentment between Poles and Irish is, in many instances, far more serious than are their feelings toward any of the heretics, schismatics, infidels, agnostics and apostates (all currently called separated brothers) outside the Church. The lines among the various Catholic ethnic groups may be growing a bit more blurred, but they are still there, and any bishop who forgets it and sends an Irish priest to a Polish parish, or vice versa, is not going to be able to forget it for very long.

I would make two assertions about the relationship between religion and ethnicity.

1) The ethnic groups provide subdivisions and subdefinitions within the various religious communities. Catholicism is, for example, still too big a category to be completely satisfactory—at least for everyone—as a quasi-communal identification.

2) There is a two-way flow of influence between religion and ethnicity. From one point of view it can truly be said that the Irish are Catholic because they are Irish. That is, the identification of Catholicism with Irish nationalism has helped to make the Irish the strong, if not to say militant, Catholics that they are. On the other hand, the fact that the Irish in the United States are Catholic and are linked to the Catholic Church through the Irish tradition probably makes them more likely to be conscious of their Irish origins than they would be if religion and ethnicity were not so intimately linked in their cultural experience. Whether it is religion or ethnicity that is celebrated during the St. Patrick's Day parade is anyone's guess, but I think we can say, with some degree of safety, that it is both, and that the nature of the relationships and of the mix between the relationships is likely to vary from individual to individual.

Ethnic groups—even if they are not subcultures (and I suspect they are)—are at least substructures of the larger society, and in some cities, comprehensive substructures. The Polish community in Chicago, for example; the Jewish community in New York; the Irish community in Boston; the black community of Harlem all represent a pool of preferred associates so vast and so variegated that it is possible, if one chooses, to live almost entirely within the bounds of the community. One can work with, play with, marry, attend church with, vote with and join fraternal organizations with people who are of exactly the same ethnic background. One can choose fellow ethnics to perform all the professional functions one requires, from interior decorator to psychiatrist to undertaker. One can belong to ethnic organizations, read ethnic newspapers, seek counsel from ethnic clergymen, play on ethnic baseball teams and vote for ethnic candidates in elections. While some of us may lament the exclusiveness in such ethnic communities, it is nonetheless true that the pattern of ethnic relationships constitutes an important part of the fabric of the larger community, organizing the amorphous population of the city into a number of clearly identifiable and elaborately structured subgroups.

Substructures and Life Styles

From the viewpoint of those responsible for the larger social structure, these organizations are particularly convenient because the leadership is readily identifiable and is generally willing to negotiate for the advantage of its own community members with an eye on the political realities in which it finds itself. (In Los Angeles, for example, citizens of different ethnic backgrounds are not organized into ethnic communities, and this is one reason Los Angeles is quite ungovernable. In Chicago, on the other hand, it is the ethnic substructures that make it still possible—though difficult—to govern.)

These same substructures also provide a greater degree of stability in personal and professional relationships, because those who are one's "own kind of people" are considered to be substantially more trustworthy and may, in fact, actually be more trustworthy than the members of out-groups. (By trustworthy here I do not mean that an Irish psychiatrist would cheat a German patient: I simply mean that a German psychiatrist might much more easily understand what his German client was talking about.)

Ethnic groups also serve as bearers of distinctive cultural reactions. Some of the research [1] on the relationship between medicine and ethnicity, for instance, indicates that Italians are much more likely to give free expression to feelings of pain than are Irish, and thus are likely to be a considerable trial to hospital personnel. The Irish, on the other hand, bear their pain grimly and bravely and may cause less trouble, but it is harder to discover how sick an Irishman really is, because he's not likely to tell you.

There are also differences in political style. Professor James Q. Wilson, of the Department of Political Science at Harvard, reports that when an Irish police officer has a choice between formal, official channels of communication and informal, unofficial channels, he will almost always choose the latter.[2] It was said of the Kennedy administration that, in addition to the titular head of the various administrative agencies, there was always someone at a slightly lower level who was "Kennedy's man" and had special contact with the White House on the affairs of that agency.

Some researchers have suggested that there is a great deal more fatalism and lack of achievement orientation among Italians than there is among white Anglo-Saxon Protestants. Blacks insist that "soul," and all the word implies in the black community, is not to be found among most white ethnic groups. And, as we shall point out in a later chapter, ethnic background also correlates strongly with occupational choice. According to unpublished NORC data, Jews are more inclined to be doctors than anyone else, while Germans, both Protestant and Catholic, overchoose engineering careers and the Irish overchoose law, political science and, more recently, the foreign service.[3]

I would like to make two not altogether facetious suggestions for research. First of all, we might take a serious look at debutante balls. In a city like Chicago there is a complex and elaborate hierarchy of debutante cotillions. The most important and best publicized is the Passavant cotillion which is sponsored allegedly to support one of the city's famous hospitals. It is basically a debutante party for the Protestant aristocracy, though occasionally a Catholic girl may make it if her father is rich enough or important enough. (One of Mayor Daley's daughters was a Passavant deb.)

The second ranking cotillion, sponsored by the Irish Catholic aristocracy (although certain non-Irish Catholics are permitted into it in much the same fashion the Passavant cotillion tolerates an occasional Catholic), is known as the Presentation Ball, and is named after the presentation of the young ladies supposedly to the Chicago Archbishop or one of his hapless auxiliaries.

But then the fun begins. There are Polish, Czech, Slovak, Ukrainian, German (Protestant and Catholic), Scandinavian, Puerto Rican and black cotillions, and by no means just one for each ethnic community. In fact, a researcher eager to find the similarities and the differences in such critically important social events could well keep himself busy for weeks on end, were his stomach and his nervous system strong enough.

It would be easier, I suspect, to study the culture of wedding celebrations. On this subject I can claim to be somewhat more of an expert than on debutante balls, since for weal or woe I never was fortunate enough to make one of the latter, but at one time in my career I was required professionally to show up at an almost infinite number of weddings. My impressions, subject to confirmation or rejection by further research, were that Irish wedding receptions were marked by drinking (and eventually, frequently by singing); Polish receptions by endless dancing; Bohemian receptions by prodigious consumption of food; and Jewish receptions by much food, and prodigious and interminable conversation.

I cite these two areas for research not merely because there is a certain amount of humor in debutante balls and different kinds of wedding celebrations, but also because I suspect that they will strike a familiar chord in the reader's memory. It seems fairly obvious, even though we have little empirical data to confirm it, that the ethnic communities, particularly in areas where they are relevant for their members, do indeed maintain traditions of their own. What some of these traditions would mean to their cousins in the old country may perhaps be another matter. Whether the County Mayo or the County Clare Irish, for example, would make any sense out of the Presentation Ball seems highly questionable.

Mobility Pyramids and Mobility Traps

One final point needs to be made about the social functions of ethnic groups: They provide mobility pyramids that may turn into mobility traps.[4] Because the ethnic subcommunity is, at least if it's big enough, a comprehensive substructure, it is possible for an upwardly mobile professional and businessman to build his career almost entirely within its confines. Not only a general practitioner, but even a surgeon, can have patients almost all of his own ethnic background; a Catholic academician can achieve a position within the system of Catholic colleges (which are, for the most part, Irish Catholic colleges) that he would not enjoy in the larger academic system; a political leader can gain far more power as the head of an ethnic faction within the party than he would if he tried to operate without such a power base; a contractor or an undertaker may do very well indeed servicing the needs of his ethnic colleagues, where he might be considerably less successful competing beyond the bounds of the ethnic group; even a racketeer, though he may be viewed with contempt by the larger society, may be respected for his success and affluence within his own substructure.

These mobility pyramids are, of course, very helpful for those who manage to achieve influence, affluence and prestige that might well be less possible for them in the larger society. And such substructural mobility probably adds to the satisfaction and morale of the members of an ethnic community. On the other hand, there is the risk of a mobility trap. A promising academician who accepts his first major appointment at a Catholic college may move up very rapidly within the Catholic system, but find the door closed to him for more meaningful mobility outside the system. Similarly, a doctor who has built his clientele within the ethnic community may feel that he has great prestige there, but when he goes to medical association meetings and finds himself outside the power elite of these associations, he may wonder if he might not have had even greater success beyond his own ethnic group.

A few individuals manage to avoid the ethnic trap, moving from positions within their own group to similar positions in the larger structure, with increased influence and prestige. Thus, certain journalists whose careers originally were established within Catholic publishing journals have been able, because of their success on these journals, to switch over to important positions with secular newspapers and magazines. And the Kennedys, whose power roots lie in the ward politics of Boston, were able—with the aid of large sums of money and great personal dedication—to break out of the Irish Catholic political mold and make it in the big time. But the mobility pitfalls persist, and many ethnics eager for upward mobility are faced with Caesar's choice—whether to be first in the small pyramid or run the risk of being second (or much lower than second) in Rome.

In summary, then, the functions of ethnic groups in American society are multiple. They keep cultural traditions alive, provide us with preferred associates, help organize the social structure, offer opportunities for mobility and success and enable men to identify themselves in the face of the threatening chaos of a large and impersonal society. On the other hand, they reinforce exclusiveness, suspicion and distrust, and, as we have already noted, serve as ideal foci for conflict. Finally, ethnic groups are something like the Rocky Mountains or the Atlantic Ocean— whether we like them or not really doesn't matter very much; they are concrete realities with which we must cope, and condemning or praising them is a waste of time.

Notes

1. Edward A. Suchmam, "Sociomedical Variation Among Ethnic Groups," *American Journal of Sociology*, 70 (November 1964), p. 319.

2. James Q. Wilson, "Generational and Ethnic Differences Among Career Police Officers," *American Journal of Sociology*, 69 (March 1964), pp. 522–28.

3. A finding which suggests that the Irish may have left behind the precinct for the Embassy.

4. In this section I lean heavily on the suggestions of Peter H. Rossi and the writings of Norbert Wiley.

Chapter 4.
Steps in Ethnic Assimilation

Anyone who is interested in peace and tranquillity within American society has wondered if interethnic peace in the United States is possible. Before we turn to this thorny question, however, we must face yet another complex of American life—the fact that the various ethnic groups which coexist with one another are at different stages in the process of acculturating and assimilating into the American environment.

Let me outline, briefly, a progression which may help us to understand something of this acculturation process. There are, as I see them, six steps in this process: 1) cultural shock; 2) organization and emergent self-consciousness; 3) assimilation of the elite; 4) militancy; 5) self-hatred and antimilitancy; and 6) emerging adjustment.

PHASE 1. CULTURAL SHOCK: In the first phase, the immigrant group has just arrived in the host society. The patterns of behavior that were established in the Old World are jolted and jarred. The old culture is felt to be under savage attack and the members of the immigrant group are frightened and disorganized. The leaders, such as they are, are not sure that they can hold their people together, and the outside society keeps up a drumfire of criticism. Almost all the newcomers are poor, and they work (when they find work) at the most menial and poorly paid tasks. (This was the plight, for example, of the Irish arriving in New York and Boston after the great famine, of the East European Jews arriving in New York at the turn of the century, of the blacks arriving in the cities of the North after the First and Second World Wars, and of the Poles arriving in Chicago at the time they were studied by W. I. Thomas and Florian Znaniecki in 1918.) Sheer survival is the only issue.

PHASE 2. ORGANIZATION AND EMERGING SELF-CONSCIOUSNESS: In the second phase, the immigrant group begins to become organized; its clergy, its precinct captains, the leaders of its fraternal organizations, its journalists, become the key figures in the communities. The immigrants are learning the language and their children are becoming "Hibernicized" in the public schools (or if one happens to be Catholic, in the Irish Catholic schools). The newcomers are clawing their way up the economic ladder and becoming semiskilled, occasionally even skilled, workers. Some of the brighter young people are embarking on professional careers. Having survived the first trauma of integration, the elite of the community now become concerned about whether that which is distinctively theirs is going to be lost in the assimilation process. The language, the culture, the religion of the Old World must somehow be preserved—although almost everyone agrees that the group must also become American. There is not much leisure and not much money, but enough for self-consciousness and ethnic pride to begin to assert themselves, and the political leaders of the community become skilled in bargaining for concessions in return.

PHASE 3. ASSIMILATION OF THE ELITE: In the third phase of the acculturation process, ambivalence begins to emerge. The immigrant group has managed to climb at least partially into the lower middle class. Its members are storekeepers, artisans, skilled workers, clerks, policemen, firemen, transit workers and militant trade unionists. Money is scrimped and saved to provide for the college education of promising young men, and even of young women, who are expected to become schoolteachers. The group's pride increases; though it is still diffident toward the world outside, there is a tinge of resentment and anger beneath the diffidence. "We may be struggling to win acceptance," they say under their breath, "but some day you'll have to bargain with us on *our* terms."

At the same time, the more talented and gifted individuals begin to break out of the ethnic mobility pyramids and find their way into the mainstream. Those who make it find it very difficult not to be ashamed of their ethnic background. (Such writers, for example, as James T. Farrell and John O'Hara demonstrate this tense social awkwardness about their own minority relationship to the intellectuals of the University of Chicago and of the eastern Protestant aristocracy.) There simply are not enough others of their own background who have also made it for the ethnic arriviste to feel at ease. No longer a part of that from which he came, neither is he fully accepted by those among whom he has arrived—on the contrary, he may occasionally find himself displayed as an interesting objet d'art.

The degree of assimilation and alienation of elites at this stage varies from group to group, even from person to person. The Kennedy clan, for example, was more or less accepted by the Harvard aristocracy and the international café society of "beautiful people"; yet it does not seem they were totally at ease in these worlds. But neither were they totally South Boston Irish; as a matter of fact, some of the most vicious criticisms of the Kennedys I have ever heard have come from Boston Irish clergymen who view the clan as somehow unfaithful to their Boston Irish roots.

PHASE 4. MILITANCY: In the fourth phase, the immigrant group has become fully middle class and even wedges toward upper middle class. It now is thoroughly, and at times violently, militant. It has sources of power; it has built up a comprehensive middle culture; it does not need the larger society (or so it thinks), and wants as little to do with it as possible. Its members are warned of the dangers of associating with the larger society, and simultaneously are urged to become better at everything that society does.

This is the time when a comprehensive structure of organizations is developed duplicating everything that exists in the larger society. Thus, American Catholicism has generated a Catholic lawyers' guild, a Catholic physicians' guild, Catholic sociological, historical and psychological societies, Catholic hospital wings, and indeed, Catholic versions of just about everything else to be found in the American culture. It is also the time of superpatriotism, when the immigrant group tries to prove it is not only as American as any other group, but more so.

The successful immigrant group now throws its power around

with little regard for the rights and feelings of others. "We were pushed around when we were powerless," its members argue, "now we're going to push back. It *was* their city, it's now *our* city, and we will run it our way, whether they like it or not." In the first three phases the immigrant group was the object of constant rejection; this rejection has been at least partially internalized, and now the group is overcompensating. It is busily demonstrating not only to the world outside, but also (especially) to itself that it is not inferior, and it is demonstrating this noisily, aggressively and uncompromisingly. Suspicion and distrust of the larger society and noisy, highly selective pride in the accomplishments of one's fellow ethnics are the order of the day. It is at this stage, one must note, that the ethnic group is most difficult to deal with and most likely to engage in conflict with other ethnic groups.[1]

PHASE 5. SELF-HATRED AND ANTIMILITANCY: In the fifth phase, the ethnic group is generating a substantial upper middle and professional class. Its young people are going to college in larger numbers and many are becoming successful and economically well-integrated members of the larger society. There is no question, as in the case of the earlier elites, of these new and much larger elites' alienating themselves from the immigrant group; but from the perspective of full-fledged members of the larger society, they are acutely embarrassed by the militancy, the narrowness, the provincialism of their own past and by the leaderships of organizations which seem to have a vested interest in keeping that past alive. Self-hatred, latent in the first three phases and hidden behind militancy in the fourth phase, finally comes out in the fifth phase, and devastating criticism is aimed at almost every aspect of one's own tradition and almost every institution which strives to keep one's culture alive. Yet, for most of the self-critics, there is no thought of abandoning the ethnic community or its culture completely. There are intense, emphatic demands for drastic and immediate modernization—demands which cannot possibly be met—and intense ambivalence toward the ethnic group. The self-critics cannot live with their ethnic background, and they cannot live without it.

PHASE 6. EMERGING ADJUSTMENT: Finally, in the sixth phase, another generation appears on the scene, securely upper middle class in its experience and equally secure in its ability to become part even of the upper class. Such a generation is quite conscious of its ethnic origin; it does not feel ashamed of it and has no desire to run from it, but neither is it willing to become militantly aggressive over its ethnicity. It cannot understand the militant defensiveness of the fourth phase or the militant self-hatred of the fifth, and sees no reason in theory or practice why it cannot be part of the larger society and still loyal to its own traditions. It is in this phase, one suspects, that Hansen's Law ("what the father forgets, the son remembers") becomes operative. There is a strong interest in the cultural and artistic background of one's ethnic tradition. Trips are made to the old country, no longer to visit one's family and friends, but out of curiosity and sometimes amused compassion at how one's grandparents and great-grandparents lived. Many elements of the ethnic traditions survive, some on the level of high culture, some in a continuation of older role expectations. The younger members of the ethnic groups, indeed, delight over these differences which they find so "interesting" and so much fun to explain to friends and classmates of other ethnic groups.

It is about this time that the members of an ethnic group that has reached the top begin to wonder why other groups, which have not moved as far along, are so noisy, raucous and militant.

If one were forced to cite examples of, let us say, the last three phases, one might guess that the American blacks are moving into phase four (militancy), and that the more recent Catholic immigrant groups, such as the Italians and the Poles, are in the middle of phase four and beginning to move beyond it. Irish and German Catholics began to move into phase five (self-hatred) at the end of the Second World War and have been engaging in an orgy of self-criticism (what Father Edward Duff has called mass masochism) ever since (a self-criticism which has been made even more cynical and pessimistic by the revolution of the Second Vatican Council). My own impression is that some of the American Irish in their twenties are moving into phase six (adaptation), and that large numbers of American Jews under forty are already in that phase.

Some Complicating Factors

The progression described above is quite clearly an oversimplification. It elevates hunches, impressions, and occasional illustrations to the level of high theory. But at the present stage of our research on ethnicity, it is the best this writer can evolve, and perhaps it will stimulate others to try for something better.

Two observations and one warning might be added: First of all, the posture of a given ethnic group in relation to the other groups is likely to change dramatically as the group moves through the acculturation-assimilation process. It is probably impossible to accelerate the process very much, but at least one can understand it and realize why, at a given time, a particular ethnic group may be very difficult to deal with. It would be wise to realize that one's ancestors were equally difficult to deal with at a somewhat earlier period in history.

The second observation is that it is probably unwise for members of outside ethnic groups to become involved in the internal conflicts that plague a group through phases three, four and five. For outsiders to encourage one set of leaders in a group is the surest way in the world to make sure those leaders are disqualified from further effective leadership. There may never before have been so descriptive and emotionally charged a phrase as "Uncle Tom," but the idea is foreign to no ethnic group; and if there are leaders in a given community with whom we are better able to get along, we are well advised not to embarrass them by pointing them out to their fellows as the most sensible of men, because that will be the end of their power.

My warning has to do with the possibility of regression. If an ethnic group feels itself attacked again, after having "made it" in the larger society, it may very well regress, at least temporarily, to an earlier stage. It should not be surprising, therefore, that some rank and file members of the Jewish community in New York are likely to feel quite violent about the threat of black anti-Semitism. Their shock and displeasure are similar to the anger of the white Protestants as later immigrant groups displaced them—though the white Protestants generally did not go through the difficult and painful process of assimilating and acculturating to a society. Since it was their society to begin with, they did not have to pay the psychic price that later immigrant groups paid, and hence are not likely to be quite so angry when someone backs them into a corner.

This outline of the stages of acculturation and assimilation provides us with a tool, admittedly crude, for understanding many of the other intergroup conflicts which plague the United States, particularly in its large cities. It also enables us to make some tentative predictions and raise some interesting questions. One such question, for example, concerns the remarkable phenomenon of the Puerto Rican experience. Some students [2] of Puerto Rican acculturation have suggested that it has taken place at a more rapid rate than that of any other group that has ever come to the United States; and while the Puerto Rican leadership has been militant, the community has rarely engaged in violence. It will be a very interesting community to watch as it moves into the final three phases we have described.

Notes

1. As we note in Chapter 14, hostile feelings seem to be increasing between Catholics and Jews, although both have presumably moved fairly well through the militancy phase. The sequence I have described does not exclude the possibility of regression.

2. Joseph Fitzpatrick, "Intermarriage of Puerto Ricans in New York," *American Journal of Sociology,* 71 (November 1966), pp. 395–406.

Chapter 5.
Competition Among Ethnic Groups

It is now time for us to concentrate on the most critical aspect of ethnic life in the United States—competition among ethnic groups—though competition is by no means the sole cause of intergroup conflict. We must assume that competition among different groups for resources that are scarce or are presumed to be scarce, is inevitable. The question is whether, and to what extent, such competition can be kept from turning into conflict.

A number of social scientists, most notably Lewis Coser, have argued that social conflict is a good thing, that it is a safety valve permitting society or groups within it to let off excess steam which, if contained, could lead to violent explosions. Coser argues that when the patterns of relationships in society are no longer adequate to the social realities, group conflict is a way of forcing a restructuring without destroying the patterns completely. Thus, if a given ethnic group has less political power than its size, group-consciousness and desires would make appropriate, conflict between this group and other groups which have more power than their size seems to warrant is a way of restructuring the social order before frustration and dissatisfaction tear it apart.

In the context of Coser's very wise theorizing, the present phase of black militancy can be seen as highly constructive for society, because it is forcing concessions to the blacks of positions, prestige, power, control and responsibility appropriate to their size, their stake in society and their emerging self-consciousness. If there were no social conflict to force this restructuring, there might be an eruption which would tear the total society apart. Although some black extremists use a rhetoric of destruction, it still seems safe to say that, thus far, black militancy seems to have restructuring rather than destruction as its goal. Such a perspective is an extremely useful one; but it is still necessary to point out either that social conflict is useful up to a point and then itself becomes destructive of the social fabric, or that there are two kinds of social conflict—that which leads to restructuring, and that which leads to destruction. Unfortunately, the two shade off one into another in such a way that it's often hard to tell which kind we are watching.

The late John Courtney Murray wrote and spoke frequently of the "conspiracies" within American society. He argued that the various religious groups were, indeed, competing for power and influence, but at least within some vaguely agreed-upon "rules of the game"—rules which everyone was careful not to make too explicit lest the very explicitness become a source for conflict. Social conflict is likely to lead to restructuring as long as there is some agreement on the rules of the game, and it is likely to lead to destruction when there is not even a vague agreement. (Some of the student unrest currently afflicting the campuses seems to be operating in a context where one can see no agreement on the rules of the game between the student extremists and the rest of the university.) The nonviolent phase of the civil rights movement operated under rather explicitly agreed upon rules of the game, and even though the nonviolent phase is now assumed to be over, a substantial segment of the black leadership, in reality if not in rhetoric, still seems willing to settle, as did other ethnic groups before them, for "more" within the existing structure.

Arenas of Conflict

Most of the conflicts between ethnic and religio-ethnic groups currently going on in American society are well within the rules of the game (one is that we may accuse other groups of breaking the rules, as long as we do not push that accusation too far). Violence may occasionally break out, especially between the races, and on the fringes where one ethnic ghetto brushes against another, either physically or psychologically. But given the size, complexity and newness of American society, the astonishing phenomenon is not that there is interethnic conflict, but that it is not more destructive.

There is, first of all, the conflict of political competition. In New York, there is the struggle between Jews and Catholics for control of the Democratic party—a struggle which has led many Jews to form what is basically their own political party, the Liberals. And among the Catholics there is conflict between the Italians and the Irish for control of the Democratic Party. The Republican Party is still basically white Protestant, though it has managed to attract some liberal Jews who find the liberal and aristocratic WASP more to their liking than either the unsophisticated Catholics of the Democrats or the socialistically oriented Jews in the Liberal Party. The blacks and the Puerto Ricans are generally within the confines of the Democratic coalition, and have been accorded some positions of power and prestige, but nowhere in keeping with their numbers. The Republicans have managed to elect a white Protestant liberal as mayor of New York; and the intelligent and sophisticated Mr. Lindsay has attracted large support from both Jews and blacks in his challenge to the Italo-Hibernian-dominated Democratic party. For a native New Yorker, this all makes a great deal of sense in a bizarre way, and for a native Chicagoan like myself, it is very understandable (though we have a hard time grasping how the New York Irish can be as inept as they are; in Chicago we are much better at playing one ethnic group off against another). But one suspects that for the native of Nebraska or Nottingham or Naples or Nantes or Nijmegen, the politics of New York City (or Boston or Chicago or Detroit) must seem like an incredibly confused jungle. To them, all we can say is, you should see what it's like in Los Angeles.

The second focus for conflict is housing. As each ethnic group improves its economic situation, it seeks new housing—at least housing that is new for it—and begins to move from its original location into neighborhoods that previously have been the preserve of other ethnic groups. Generally speaking, the first neighborhoods to be so "invaded" are already declining, either out of physical obsolescence or because the most ambitious of its citizens are already seeking better housing for themselves. But invasion by a "foreign" ethnic group is a profound threat; not only does it imply (despite overwhelming evidence to the contrary) a decline in sales value of one's own house; it also is a challenge to friendship patterns, churches, familiar landscape and shopping areas, and all those things a man has come to value in that particular area he thinks of as his own.

The conflict between white and black has been so well publicized in recent years that we tend to forget that other ethnic groups have "battled" for neighborhoods, and that such conflicts continue, even today. When I was growing up on the West Side of Chicago, an Italian family was only a little more welcome in an Irish neighborhood on the South Side than a Negro family would have been; and while the replacement of Poles by Puerto Ricans in Chicago is more peaceful than the replacement of whites by blacks, there is still tension and potential conflict in such replacement of one ethnic group by another.

Education provides another focus for interethnic conflict. Again the most obvious conflict today is between blacks and whites, over attempts to create racial balance in the public school system and the efforts of black militants to gain more and more control of the schools in their own communities (which means, in part, control over white teachers who work in these schools). But various white ethnic groups have fought among themselves for control of the public school system, with Catholics warring against Protestants and various Catholic groups fighting with each other. Catholics have generally supported religious activities in public schools (though Catholic liberals and intellectuals have opposed it); Protestants are divided on the issue and most Jews are for rigorous separation of church and state in the public schools. A similar division takes place on state support of one sort or another to religious schools, though Protestant groups would shift somewhat more against such aid, and at least some Jews would be in favor of it. Finally, within the Catholic Church, the struggle continues between the dominant Irish and other groups for control of the Catholic school system, which the Irish have generally used as an Americanizing—that is to say, Hibernicizing—force, while other immigrant groups have attempted to develop their own national Catholic schools where their culture and language are kept alive.

Ethnic battles also rage in the trade unions, where leadership, once Irish or German or Jewish, has recently shifted somewhat toward the Italians and the Slavic immigrant groups. In the meantime, the blacks have become conscious that they are un- derrepresented at the middle and higher levels of union leader- ship and are beginning to demand what they deem to be ade- quate representation in the upper councils of labor.

In the business world, particularly the world of the small shop or the small entrepreneur, such as the construction contractor, vigorous, if not to say vicious and cut-throat, competition exists along ethnic lines, though there is little documentation on the subject. Similarly, in the demimonde of the rackets, Italian (which is to say generally Sicilian) leadership has replaced the Irish and the occasional Jewish leadership of years gone by, but now finds itself beginning to be threatened by restless black al- lies.

The Struggle for Power

Politics, housing, religion, education, unions, business—indeed in almost any area in American life where conflict is possible— the ethnic groups form temporary shifting alliances as their members struggle to obtain more power or to preserve the power they already have. Differences in religion and social class may exacerbate the conflict situations and the apparently inevi- table human inclination to question the good faith of those who are different makes the conflict potential even worse. The suspi- cion, if not hatred, for example, of a Jewish or Protestant intel- lectual and liberal for the Irish politician has by no means dis- appeared from the American scene.

Hatred for that which is different apparently still lurks just beneath our civilized veneer. We are not yet that very far from the tribal state, and while necessity keeps most of us to the rules of the game, we are deeply suspicious that members of other groups will violate those rules at the first opportunity.

Some of the conflict situations we have mentioned are purely ethnic: for example, the struggle between the Irish and other na- tionality groups for control inside the Catholic Church, while other conflicts—black against white, Jew versus Catholic—are ethnic and racial or religious. While it is difficult in our present state of knowledge to sort out the influence of race, ethnicity and religion, it is not particularly important, for practical purposes, that we do so. But we must remember that it is not merely religious theory that keeps Catholics and Jews suspicious of each other, nor merely racial history that created the school problem in New York City. The struggle between Catholic and Jew over the public schools, for example, is not so much rooted in religious differences as in the political and social styles of two immigrant groups jockeying for prestige and power in an urban world where they are closely juxtaposed. Only if we understand that the battle is between two ethnic groups searching for more power themselves, but afraid to give the distrusted foe any more power lest he use it against them, can we understand the depth of the passions and fears involved.

Theoretical positions on civil rights made blacks and Jews close allies for a long time; but today they are often at odds. Yet, it is not racism that is the issue, save very indirectly. Rather, it is a struggle between two immigrant groups for what both think is their proper share of the urban power pie.

In both the Catholic-Jewish and the Negro-Jewish conflicts, of course, religion and race are involved in many different ways, but I am suggesting that even if these two factors could be drained out of the conflict, the basic resentment toward a group of "strangers" who are trying to take something from us, or keep something from us that is rightfully ours, will make the conflict almost as serious as it is at the present time.

Chapter 6.
"We" and "They": The Differences Linger

We now turn from speculation and theory about ethnicity to some concrete data about differences among ethnic groups in America. I think they help establish the fact that we are not just idly speculating when we say that ethnic groups have survived in the United States, and continue to be the bearers of different cultural traditions. In addition, I think they may provide us with some hints as to the problems that ethnic differences seem to portend for American society, as well as some clues to further research that might be appropriate.

The data described stem from three major sources: first, a national survey of American Catholics [1] done in 1963; second, data about the attitudes of June 1961 college graduates seven years after graduation (collected as part of a long-term study of education and careers by the National Opinion Research Center of the University of Chicago); [2] and finally, information obtained from a study of urban neighborhoods undertaken in 1967, also by the National Opinion Research Center.[3]

The 1963 Catholic Survey

From the 1963 survey (Table 4) we learn that the Irish, first arrivals among American Catholics, are the most successful group as measured by their education, as well as by the prestige of their jobs [4] and their income. They also score highest on measures of general knowledge, are the most open-minded and the most likely to exhibit high morale, as gauged both by measures of happiness [5] and of anomie, i.e., the state of disorientation, anxiety and isolation that develops when standards of conduct and belief have weakened or disappeared. They are the most pious and least given to religious extremism, racism [6] or anti-Semitism.[7]

TABLE 4
SELECTED ATTRIBUTES OF CATHOLIC
ETHNIC GROUPS IN U.S.

	Irish	Germans	Italians	Poles	French
Have completed high school	77%	62%	51%	46%	42%
Hold prestige jobs	32	31	13	17	22
Earn over $14,000 a year	24	19	17	18	7
Belong to Democratic Party	70	65	67	77	70
Score high on general knowledge	18	9	7	3	5
Score high on open-mindedness	52	48	42	43	40
Consider themselves "very happy"	41	36	35	27	40
Score low on anomie	64	51	47	43	49
Score high on piety	32	31	13	30	22
Score high on religious extremism	19	20	24	34	28
Score high on racism	44	46	54	61	51
Score high on anti-Semitism	29	47	43	52	54
(Number of persons interviewed)	(328)	(361)	(370)	(184)	(177)

The Catholic German-Americans are almost as successful as the Irish in occupational status, though not in education or income. They are only slightly less devout than the Irish, slightly more given to religious extremism, somewhat less secure in their personal morale and somewhat less open-minded.

Italians and Poles, both more recent Catholic immigrants, have yet to achieve the educational, occupational and financial success of their Irish and German predecessors, and score lower in happiness and open-mindedness. They score higher on measures of racism than the older groups, but while the Poles also score higher on anti-Semitism, the Italians are lower on anti-Semitism even than the Germans. Poles are most likely, and Italians (together with Germans) least likely, to be members of

TABLE 5
SELECTED ATTRIBUTES OF CATHOLIC ETHNIC GROUPS
IN U.S.—HIGH-SCHOOL GRADUATES OF THIRD
OR LATER GENERATION ONLY

	Irish	Germans	Italians	Poles	French
Hold prestige jobs	31%	34%	12%	32%	21%
Work as professionals or managers	45	47	37	22	31
Earn over $14,000 a year	26	22	3	21	11
Belong to Democratic Party	67	61	51	62	76
Score high on general knowledge	26	17	20	11	9
Score high on open-mindedness	51	56	51	34	40
Consider themselves "very happy"	47	38	26	32	48
Score low on anomie	74	60	44	61	60
Score high on piety	32	32	10	20	39
Score high on religious extremism	14	15	20	31	26
Score high on racism	39	30	54	61	29
Score high on anti-Semitism	25	38	32	59	43
(Number of persons interviewed)	(131)	(102)	(29)	(24)	(31)

the Democratic Party. And whereas Italians are the least pious of all the Catholic groups, the Poles are almost as devout as the Irish.

Finally, French Americans [8] are among the least pious of American Catholic groups, second only to Poles with respect to religious extremism, and highest of all groups on measures of anti-Semitism. They score almost as high as the Irish in happiness, but they tend a good deal more toward anomie.

Can these differences be explained away, perhaps, by the fact that some of the Catholic ethnic groups have been in this country longer than others, or become better educated? The way to check this is to compare only individuals of the same generation and educational level—for example, those who are at least third-generation Americans and have completed high school (Table 5). We then find that the typical differences between ethnic groups tend to diminish, but that many of them persist at least in some degree.

Thus, in occupational prestige and income the Irish and Germans are still the most successful, though the Poles have just about pulled abreast. The Irish still rank highest in general knowledge, with Italians now in second place and Germans in third. The Italians now are even more likely than the Germans to have left the Democratic Party. Poles again score high on anti-Semitism and racism, and both Poles and Italians continue to score low on happiness. The Irish and French are again the happiest, putting to rest (forever, I hope) the notion that the Celts are a morose and melancholy lot. I shall leave to others to explain why the descendants of sunny Italy seem so gloomy in this instance—though with only twenty-nine of them in the table; one could easily argue that the whole sample must have been made up of sombre Milanese.

The findings of the 1963 survey were sorted out according to region as well as generation, with at least one striking result: The Poles' high scores on measures of anti-Semitism and racism were limited to the Midwest. Poles on the East Coast did not differ from other Catholics in these respects. It seems reasonable to conclude, therefore, that while ethnic differences persist even after three or four generations and among the better educated, the shape and direction of these differences is affected by various other factors—economic, social or geographical. In all likelihood, the heavier the concentration of an ethnic group in a given area, the more likely it is to form a tight ethnic community and to take a negative attitude toward outsiders.

Are the differences presented in Table 5 "pure ethnic" differences or can they be explained by the different educational, occupational and generational backgrounds of members of the different ethnic groups? The answer is that both factors seem to be at work. In Table 6 we convert the percentages of Table 5 into mean scores in order that the complex multiple regression mode of analysis may be used.[9]

TABLE 6
DIFFERENCES AMONG CERTAIN AMERICAN MALES

Ethnic groups°	Irish	German	Italian	Poles
Mean years in school	12.98	11.60	11.20	11.25
Mean occupational prestige (1–100)	44.2	36.2	34.8	32.2
Mean family income	$8,530	$8,059	$8,159	$8,219
Mean score on general knowledge scale (0–8)	5.17	4.33	4.16	4.32
Mean score on racism scale (0–5)	2.42	2.45	2.60	2.61
Mean score on anti-Semitism scale (0–2)	.84	1.23	1.11	1.71
(Number of persons interviewed)	(138)	(153)	(182)	(80)

° Father's main ethnic background.

In Table 7 the Germans, Italians and Poles are compared in educational, occupational, financial achievement and social attitude with the Irish. The first line in each gives the gross differences in achievement between the Irish and the other three groups while the second line in each panel states the net difference when the impact of background factors has been filtered out. Thus, in panel 7a we see that most of the educational difference between the Italians and Irish can be explained in terms of parental education, occupation and generation and that, furthermore, these three factors substantially reduce the differences be-

TABLE 7a
DIFFERENCES IN EDUCATIONAL ACHIEVEMENT
BETWEEN IRISH ETHNICS AND
OTHER ETHNIC GROUPS

	German	Italian	Poles
Gross differences in years of education	1.38	1.78	1.73
Net differences when father's education, father's occupation and generation are taken into account	.95	.05	.26

TABLE 7b
DIFFERENCES IN OCCUPATIONAL PRESTIGE
BETWEEN IRISH AND OTHER ETHNIC GROUPS

	German	Italian	Poles
Gross differences in prestige scores	8.0	9.4	12.2
Net differences when father's occupation and education, generation and own education are taken into account	—.2	3.9	6.9

TABLE 7c
DIFFERENCES IN 1963 FAMILY INCOME BETWEEN IRISH
AND OTHER ETHNIC GROUPS

	German	Italian	Poles
Gross differences	$471	$331	$311
Net differences when father's occupation and education, generation, own education and own occupation are taken into account	—166	—739	356

TABLE 7d
DIFFERENCES IN RACISM SCORE
(0–5)

	German	Italian	Poles
Mean	.031	.140	.189
Father's education and occupation; own education and occupation and 1963 income	—.217	—.028	.197

TABLE 7e
DIFFERENCES IN ANTI-SEMITISM SCORES

	German	Italian	Poles
Mean	.394	.273	.871
Father's education and occupation and own education and occupation and 1963 family income	.271	.235	.698

tween the Irish and the Poles but that there is still, even with these background factors taken into account, almost a year's net difference in educational achievement between the Irish and the Germans.

Furthermore, in Table 7b we see that differences in occupational prestige between the Germans and the Irish are eliminated when parental occupation, education, generation and respondent's own education are taken into account. On the other hand, while the differences between the Irish and the Italians and Poles are reduced by half, the differences do in fact remain. It is worth noting that this difference means that even among those with exactly the same kind of education the Irish have somewhat higher prestige occupations than do the Italians or the Poles.

In Table 7c we observe something of a turnaround. Among Germans and Italians from the same parental background with the same education and with the same kind of occupation there are in fact higher income levels ($166 more per year for the Germans and $739 more per year for the Italians) than for comparable American Irish but, on the other hand, Poles with the same background make less money than do the Irish and over a $1,000 less per year than do the Italians. As Spaeth and I note in the articles, "If the variations reported . . . should persist when analysis becomes possible with more extensive data than are currently available to us, the finding would indeed be astonishing. We would have to conclude that Italians with similar family backgrounds, similar education and similar occupation make more money (approximately $700 more) than do Irish, while Poles make $358 less than the Irish do. If these differences do persist with further research, American social science will have a very knotty problem. While superior language skills might explain why the Irish make more money than the Poles, no such explanation is available for explaining why the Irish makes less than the Italians."

A somewhat similar pattern emerges in Table 7d. When father's education and occupation, one's own education, one's own occupation and one's own income are all held constant, Germans and Italians actually have lower scores on the scale measuring racism than do the Irish. On the other hand, holding constant all these background variables actually increases the difference between the Poles and the Irish in their racism score.

Finally, in Table 7 we note that control for all the background variables decreases somewhat the difference in mean scores between the Irish and the other three groups but, even with all these differences held constant, Germans, Italians and Poles still score higher in measures of anti-Semitism than do the Irish.

In other words, education, occupation, economic achievement and social attitudes are different among the four American ethnic groups on which we have data and some of these differences do persist—though in patterns difficult to explain—even when background influences are filtered out.

The Study of College Graduates

The National Opinion Research Center's study of June 1961 college graduates, and their attitudes seven years after graduation, was not limited to Catholics; hence it provides information about a substantial number of ethnic groups. (See Table 8 in Appendix.)

One of the factors touched on was political affiliations. According to the findings, Jews are most likely to belong to the Democratic Party, and Protestants least likely. Polish Jews are more likely to be Democrats than German Jews, and Irish Catholics are more likely to be Democrats than German or Italian Catholics. (See Table 9 in Appendix.)

The Jews and the Irish score as less likely than any other ethnic group to hold racist ideas, with the Scandinavians and the Poles just behind them. Other groups tend to be substantially more prejudiced, with the Protestant Germans ranking highest among the lot on measures of racism.[10]

As one might expect, Jews score higher on measures of reading and cultural interests than do Protestants, and Protestants score generally higher than Catholics—although Germans, both Protestant and Catholic, are the least likely to report intensive reading habits. German Jews seem to have more intense reading and cultural interests than Polish Jews; the Scandinavians lead the Protestants, and the Irish score highest among the Catholics. Polish Catholics, however, are most likely to plan a career in academia, followed by German Jews, Protestant Scandinavians and Catholic Irish. Protestant and Catholic Germans, together with Italians, are least likely to plan academic careers. (See Tables 13 and 14 in Appendix.)

The differences among the college graduates are, in their own way, even more striking than the differences among the general population; for the college graduates are all young, well educated and (one assumes) thoroughly American. And a college education does indeed seem to change some things—Polish attitudes toward blacks, for example, apparently improve very considerably as the result of higher education. Yet differences of 20 to 30 percentage points persist in many other measurements of attitude and behavior, despite college training. Fifty-one percent of the Catholic Irish were willing to agree with the Kerner Commission's conclusion that white racism was the cause of Negro riots in cities, for example, while only 34 percent of their German coreligionists would vote the same way (Table 8). Thirty-seven percent of the Protestant Scandinavians could accept the Kerner Commission's conclusions, but only 28 percent of their German confreres were willing to agree with them.

TABLE 8
RACIAL ATTITUDES AMONG COLLEGE GRADUATES
OF DIFFERENT RELIGIOUS AND ETHNIC BACKGROUNDS
(June 1961 graduates, surveyed in 1968)

"White racism is the cause of Negro riots in the city"

	Proportion agreeing		*Proportion agreeing*
Blacks	84%	Catholic Italians	35%
German Jews	54	Catholic Germans	34
Catholic Irish	51	Protestant English	30
Polish Jews	43	Protestant Irish	28
Catholic Poles	43	Protestant Germans	28
Protestant Scandinavians	37		

Turning from racism to another measure of attitudes on contemporary social problems, an index of sympathy with student militancy, we find a similar pattern (see Table 11 in Appendix). The Jews and the blacks are the most sympathetic; the Irish are the most sympathetic among the Catholics, but only slightly ahead of the Poles; and the Scandinavians are the most sympathetic of the Protestants—in fact, of all white Christians. Germans, both Catholic and Protestant, are the least sympathetic within their respective religious traditions.

Regional differences, or differences in the size of the localities in which the respondents live, may explain many of the differences reported here. Yet the geographical distribution of, let us say, the Irish Catholic, Italian Catholic and Polish Catholic population is such that region or locale cannot account for all of the differences. (Neither, of course, can social class, since all the respondents are college graduates.) The socialization experience of higher education has not eliminated ethnic group differences in attitudes and behavior, even among the Scandinavians and the Germans, whose geographic distribution is similar, or among the Irish, Italian and Polish Catholics, who share a common religion.

In the college graduate study a further analysis was made to

TABLE 9
SCORE ON SCALE MEASURING SYMPATHY
FOR POLITICAL MILITANCY
(June 1961, College Graduates Responding in 1968)   (Scale: 0-18)

All	9.5	
		(4,324)
Jews	11.9	
		(100)
Catholics		
Irish	10.6	
		(269)
German	9.2	
		(280)
Polish	10.5	
		(54)
Italian	8.3	
		(168)

see whether differences among ethnic groups in attitudes towards the student and black protest persisted even among those who have gone to graduate school. The various items measuring attitudes towards student and black protest were combined into a scale measuring "sympathy for political militancy." In Table 9 we note that Jews, Irish Catholics and Poles are more sympathetic to such militancy than the general population of June 1961, graduates. Germans have about the same level of sympathy as does the whole population of alumni and Italians are a full point lower on the scale than the average (and two points lower than the Irish and the Poles).

Furthermore, we also observe in Table 10 that while sympathy with militancy goes up with graduate school education, the relative differences among the groups remain pretty much the same, with the Jews, the Irish and the Polish being most sympathetic to militancy and the Italians the least sympathetic.[11]

The Neighborhood Study

The 1967 study of urban neighborhoods indicates that there are considerable differences in neighborhood behavior among Amer-

TABLE 10
SCORE ON SCALE WITH NUMBER OF YEARS
IN GRADUATE SCHOOL HELD CONSTANT

	Under one year	One or two years	Three or more years
All alumni	7.8	9.9	11.5
	(1,803)	(1,211)	(1,316)
Jews	10.3	10.9	13.2
	(29)	(21)	(50)
Catholics			
Irish	8.6	11.4	11.9
	(92)	(70)	(107)
German	8.5	8.9	10.8
	(160)	(44)	(84)
Polish	9.4	10.4	11.7
	(20)	(15)	(19)
Italian	6.4	9.7	9.8
	(73)	(49)	(46)

ican groups. The findings (see Tables 19 and 20 in Appendix) show that Jews most often belong to neighborhood organizations and engage in a considerable amount of socializing, while the Poles score lowest on the socializing scale. Italians are least likely to belong to organizations (though they are most likely to describe themselves as very sociable). The Irish most frequently state that they enjoy everything in their neighborhood and worry little, while both the Italians and the Jews score high on measures of worry. But the Italians, while they admit to worrying, also claim more often than the Jews or any Protestants that they are enjoying themselves. It would seem, then, that the Irish and the Germans are low worriers and high enjoyers, while the Italians are high worriers and high enjoyers.

Perhaps the most significant findings in the neighborhood study have to do with where people live and how frequently they associate with members of their families (Table 11; see also Tables 21 and 22 in Appendix). Of all the ethnic groups Italians most often live in the same neighborhood as their parents and siblings and visit them every week; together with the Poles and French, they also live most frequently near their in-laws or see

TABLE 11
FAMILY RELATIONSHIPS OF RELIGIOUS AND ETHNIC GROUPS

	Live in same neighborhood with			See weekly		
	Parents	Siblings	In-laws	Parents	Siblings	In-laws
Catholics						
Italians	40%	33%	24%	79%	61%	62%
Irish	17	16	16	49	48	48
Germans	10	13	10	48	31	41
Poles	29	25	24	65	46	53
French	15	23	24	61	41	62
Protestants						
English	19	13	12	39	26	35
Germans	12	13	14	44	32	39
Scandi-						
navians	14	11	17	39	26	31
Jews	14	12	14	58	33	58

them weekly. Protestants as a group are less likely than Catholics to live in the same neighborhood with relatives and to visit them weekly. Jews, though no more likely than Protestants to live in the same neighborhoods, are more likely to visit their parents weekly than any of the Protestants, or the Irish and German Catholics.

When the same data are sorted out according to social class and the physical distance that separates the respondents from parents and relatives, an extremely interesting finding emerges. Italians are still the most likely to visit both their parents and their siblings. The Jews are now in second place in visits to parents, but at the bottom of the list where visits to siblings are concerned. The Irish, on the other hand, are relatively low on the parent-visiting list, but right behind the Italians in visits to siblings. It would seem that the stereotypes of the tight Italian family, the dominating Jewish parent and the clannish Irish sib group are, at least to some extent, backed up by hard statistics.

Since relationships with parents and siblings play a major role in the formation of personality, it seems reasonable to suggest that the different patterns experienced by these three ethnic groups in the earliest years of life help make for quite different personality traits. If this be true, we can expect the subtle differences among the various ethnic groups to persist into the future.

Previous studies of Italian Americans, principally by Herbert Gans,[12] indicate that the familial peer group—siblings and other relatives of one's own age—are the most important influence on lower-class Italians. To some extent, data in the surveys cited above confirm Gans's findings. The Italian's relationships with his parents seem to be a function of physical proximity; with his siblings, the bond overcomes even physical separation. However, Gans suggests that this sibling closeness is essentially working-class and not Italian behavior, whereas in our findings the ethnic differences seem to persist even when different social classes are examined separately.

It is extremely difficult to tie together the diverse data from the various studies cited into a coherent pattern. But the information summarized above allows us to attempt the following generalizations:

The earlier immigrant groups are both the most socially successful and the most tolerant, but there are enough differences between, say, the Irish and the Germans, or between the Italians and the Poles, to suggest that other factors are at work besides the time at which one's parents washed up on American shores.

Of all the ethnic and religious groups the Jews are politically the most liberal and socially the most active, as well as economically the most successful. They are close to their parents, relatively less close to their siblings, and given to worrying.

Italians are conservative in their child-rearing practices and extremely close to their relatives—to their parents basically because they live close to them, but to their siblings, apparently, because the sibling relationship is very important to them. They are only moderately successful socially and economically, relatively uninvolved in organizational activity (perhaps because of their heavy family commitment) and liberal on some political questions, though more likely to leave the Democratic Party than are other Catholic ethnic groups. Though they think of themselves as very sociable, they are likely to have a lot of worries. They score rather low in measures of canonical religiousness, and fairly high on prejudice, though not as high as the Poles or the French. A college education apparently reduces, but does not completely eliminate, these differences in degree of prejudice.

The Irish are economically and socially the most successful among Catholic immigrant groups and the most liberal politically and socially. They have very strong ties with their siblings, are the most devoutly Catholic, and the least prejudiced, and their view of themselves ranks them as the happiest and most self-confident.

The Poles score lowest, economically and socially, of all Catholic immigrant groups, and those among them who live in the Midwest and have not graduated from college are the most likely to be prejudiced. They are very loyal to the Catholic

Church (but in a more "ethnic" way than the Irish or the Germans). They are the most likely to be Democrats and, if they are college graduates, to be liberal Democrats. They are low in morale and sociability, and high on measures of anomie.

The many historical, sociological and psychological processes that are involved in producing these differences are still frustratingly obscure, but to me they constitute one of the most fascinating questions for social research still open in our culture.

Notes

1. For a detailed discussion of the methodology of this survey, see *The Education of Catholic Americans* by Andrew M. Greeley and Peter H. Rossi (Chicago: Aldine, 1966).

2. The graduates were interviewed for the fifth time in the spring of 1968, under a grant from the Carnegie Commission on the Future of Higher Education.

3. Since the facts tread in the sensitive area of ethnic differences, a word of explanation is appropriate: The three studies cited were national sample surveys, carried out by the most careful professional methods. Although the number of respondents in each ethnic group may seem quite small to readers unfamiliar with survey research, they are, for the most part, large enough to provide some confidence that the respondents were representative of the total population. (Note carefully that the words I use are "some confidence," not absolute certainty.) The reader should be warned, however, that none of the surveys were done with ethnic research explicitly in mind. We are using questions that were designed for other purposes to seek out information about American ethnic groups. No claim can be made that the differences reported are conclusive, nor that the speculations derived from the statistical tables are more than tentative. One wishes very much that better data were available.

4. "Prestige jobs," in this context, means jobs in categories eight through ten of the Duncan Occupational Scale. This scale divides American occupational groups into ten categories according to their prestige as perceived by the total population.

5. The "happiness" measure is based on a classic survey research item which asks if respondents feel very happy, pretty happy or not too happy.

6. Racism was measured by asking respondents whether they agreed strongly, agreed somewhat, disagreed somewhat or disagreed strongly with the following statements: 1. "Negroes shouldn't push themselves where they are not wanted." 2. "White people have a right to live in an all-white

neighborhood if they want to, and Negroes should respect that right." 3. "I would strongly disapprove if a Negro family moved next door to me." 4. "Negroes would be satisfied if it were not for a few people who stir up trouble." 5. "There is an obligation to work toward the end of racial segregation."

7. Anti-Semitism was measured by asking respondents whether they agreed strongly, agreed somewhat, disagreed somewhat or disagreed strongly with these statements: 1. "Jews have too much power in the United States." 2. "Jewish businessmen are about as honest as other businessmen."

8. Most of the "French" in the sample are French-Canadian Catholics from NORC's Manchester, New Hampshire, primary sampling unit.

9. Tables 6, 7, 8 and 9 are adapted from an article by Joe L. Spaeth and me which will appear in "Stratification, Poverty and Social Conflict in American White Ethnic Groups," in *Stratification and Poverty*, edited by Seymour Martin Lipset and Michael Miller. The reader interested in more of the technical details is referred to that article.

10. I hope Polish critics of an earlier presentation of these data will note carefully my assertion that Poles who graduated from college in 1961 are considerably less likely to be prejudiced than many other American ethnics. Of the ten ethnic groups under consideration in the college graduate study, the Poles ranked seventh in racist attitudes.

11. By Table 10 the case basis becomes for most categories so thin that one hesitates to report the figures as anything more than "interesting." I trust that just as Polish readers will not accuse me of being anti-Polish for reporting the data on Polish anti-Semitism, so Italian readers will not accuse me of being anti-Italian for reporting the data on less favorable Italian attitudes towards militancy. It is worth noting, by the way, that while the Polish national population appeared conservative in the data reported in the previous section, the Polish alumni appear quite liberal in the data reported in this section. But I wish to emphasize once again that a social scientist reports findings with all the caution that sample survey research requires and with full awareness that larger samples may cause him to reverse his conclusions. Editorial writers in ethnic papers who become irate, not to say vicious, when faced with the tables presented in this chapter betray the fact that they understand neither principles of population sampling nor the tentative nature of social science research.

12. Herbert Gans, *The Urban Villagers* (Glencoe, Ill.: The Free Press, 1962).

Chapter 7.
Religion and Ethnicity

The relationship between religion and ethnicity is subtle, nor is our understanding of the relationship aided by a persistent tendency in recent American social science to see them as opposed to one another. The tendency is apparently rooted in Will Herberg's classic, *Protestant, Catholic, Jew;* he argued that America was developing a triple melting pot in which the old ethnic traditions were breaking down and three new superethnic groups —Protestant, Catholic and Jewish—were emerging. There is, of course, an immense amount to be said in favor of Herberg's model. Ethnic intermarriage is increasing despite the fact that religious intermarriage apparently is not increasing. Herberg's insight that the three major religious groups played an ethnic group function was extremely important, although it would seem now that his prediction of the vanishing of nationality groups was premature. Nonetheless, his "quasi-evolutionary" model of ethnic groups merging into religioethnic denominations fit in perfectly with the assumption of American social science that nationality background was no longer an important variable in American society. Herberg's point that the religious denominations *were* ethnic seems to have been overlooked in the enthusiasm to endorse his view that nationality groups were on the wane.

A more fruitful way of viewing the situation is to acknowledge that religion and ethnicity are intertwined, that religion plays an ethnic function in American society and ethnicity has powerful religious overtones. Like most simple evolutionary models, Herberg's was extremely useful up to a point, but beyond that point it obscured rather than clarified the situation.

While this is not the place for a treatise in the sociology of religion, one can say that religion plays two important social functions: It provides both meaning and belonging. It gives man a world view which enables him to cope with the ultimate problems of life and at the same time provides him with an ethos which gives him basic guidelines on how to live. Furthermore, as an ultimate value system shared with others, it provides a primordial "cement" which can hold human groups together. In one-religion societies, religion is *the* social cement that unifies the society. In multireligion societies like our own, the religious denomination provides a community or at least a collectivity within which its members can find some sort of answers to the ultimate questions and a group of people with which they can identify themselves. The various religions in a denominational society like our own are apt to cooperate to such an extent that an overarching social consensus is possible among the members of that society: Will Herberg's "Religion of Americanism" or Robert Bellah's "Civic Religion." Religion, therefore, can provide both social integration for a whole society and personality integration for the individual as part of that society.

In another volume [1] I have argued that Americans are less likely to question the interpretive scheme, the "meaning" of their religions, because in their society religious denomination is a strong force creating a social location and an identity for them. A denominational society—that is to say, a society where one religion is not "official" or at least a religion of the overwhelming majority—creates a situation in which denominational affiliation provides a means for defining oneself over against the other members of the society. Precisely in those societies where there is religious pluralism can one find the most vigorous church affiliation. If one looks at the various denominational societies, Holland, Canada and the United States, for example, one sees that religion is much stronger and more dynamic in these countries than it is in "one church" societies such as England or Spain or the Scandinavian countries.

The critics of American religion leap up almost at once to say that therefore American religion is "inauthentic" or a "culture religion" because it is reinforced by social pressures. But, as Clifford Geertz has pointed out, it is simply incorrect to say that social pressures prevent a religion from being authentic. A religion in a country where the social forces have emptied the churches (such as France or England) is by that reason no more "authentic" than religion in a country where the social forces have filled the churches (such as Ireland and the United States). From the viewpoint of the sociologist, in both countries those who are religious obtain meaning and belonging from their religious affiliation. Whether there is more religious "authenticity" in a denominational society than in the one church society—authenticity defined as the best in a religious tradition—is not immediately apparent to the social scientist. But a denominational society like the United States provides a host of self-critical institutions—newspapers, magazines, university professors, seminary faculties—which probably make possible a great deal more vital and "prophetic" religion than one can find in a society where social forces have weakened the church almost to the point of ineffectiveness.

We need only push this thesis a step further to say that the denominational societies tend to be ethnic societies or geographically divided societies or both. The cantons of Switzerland, the province of Quebec, the various provinces of Holland, the North and the South of Ireland and the different geographic regions of the United States are all sufficient evidence that the boundaries of geography, nationality and religion tend to coincide. There are some English Protestants in Quebec, and even some English Catholics. There are some Jews and Irish Catholics in the southwest part of the United States. There are a very considerable number of Catholics in the Protestant canton of Geneva. Ten percent of the city of Dublin is Protestant and there are, as everyone knows, a number of Catholics in the North of Ireland. However, the coincidence of these three factors is by no means accidental.

Land, religion and blood are primordial human ties. The tendency for a people with a common ancestry to have the same religion and occupy the same land is powerful and perhaps rooted in the nature of the human condition. Quite apart from doctrinal differences, liturgical variety and ethical disagreements, religious differences are profoundly important precisely because they are *ethnic*. They define *us* over against *them*.

It is easy to rail against this religious diversity. For it has normally meant disunity and frequently meant conflict and violence. However, it also means variety and richness. In any event, it seems unlikely to disappear. I see no hope at the present time that American ecumenism will ever be anything more than denominational ecumenism even though some of the mainstream Anglo-Saxon Protestant denominations may merge in COCU (Consultation on Church Unity). The main challenges, I suspect, are not to eliminate religious diversity but rather to limit the hostility and conflict it generates and to learn ways in which religious diversity can be used to facilitate richness and variety, rather than conflict and hostility.

Early American society was denominational from the very beginning. The various Protestant sects in New England, the Quakers in Pennsylvania, the Anglicans and later the Methodists in the South, found themselves against one another on religious, geographic and socioeconomic lines even though almost all were from the same Anglo-Saxon nationality background. However, even by revolutionary times, other groups had begun to arrive, especially the Irish [2] and the Germans, and, shortly thereafter, the French.

The new immigrants who came after the establishment of the nation, found that they were being defined by the whole society in terms of their religion and their nationality background. Irish Catholic, German Lutheran, Polish Catholic, German Jew, Russian Jew, religion and nationality became so intermingled in the minds of both the immigrants and the hosts that the two factors could scarcely be separated. Whether the Irish were Catholic because they were Irish, or Irish because they were Catholic is a question that is impossible to answer. It is more relevant to observe that the Irish Catholic mode of acculturation to American society was different from that of the German and both, in turn, were different from that of the Pole or the Italian. The differences between Russian and German Jews persisted for a long time and perhaps persist to some extent even today.

The result of this complex turn of social history is that religion is ethnic in the United States. One of its principal functions is to provide self-definition and social location in group cohesiveness. It interacts with nationality, to some extent with geography, in complex ways. It does not follow that intermarriage across nationality lines eliminates ethnic groups, for even the products of intermarriage frequently decide to choose one ethnic or another to affiliate with. A more helpful way of looking at the situation is to say that some Americans choose religion as their principal, primordial means of self-definition, while others choose nationality and still others choose some sort of subtle combination of both. The relevant issue for social research is not whether one replaces the other or even whether these factors are being replaced by yet other means of self-definition. The important question is, rather, under what sets of circumstances, which kinds of people find what sources of self-definition pertinent. When, for example, do I choose, explicitly or implicitly, to define myself as Irish, when as Catholic, when as Irish Catholic, when as an academic, when a Chicagoan, when as an American? Such a functional model labors under disadvantages when compared with evolutionary models. It does not help us very much to project the future or even to explain the past. However, it may be far more useful for understanding of the present.

In the United States at present two points are worth comment:

1. The persistence of a relatively high level of denominational homogeneity in marriage in the denominational society, and

2. The shifting patterns of marriage across nationality lines.

Most research done on religious intermarriage lumps all Protestant denominations together, if only because it requires very large samples to make possible the distribution of Protestants into the various denominations. The evidence in these studies seems to indicate that Jews are the least likely to marry members of other faiths, Catholics most likely and Protestants somewhere in between. However, the release of the tabulations of the 1957 Current Population Survey of Religion enables us to determine rates of religious intermarriage for a number of the Protestant denominations. The first row in Table 12 provides the rather striking information that approximately four-fifths of the members of each of the four Protestant denominations are married to people whose present religious affiliation is the same as their own. Not only are Protestants married to other Protestants, as previous studies have shown, but they are married to Protestants who share the same denominational affiliation. And the ratio of mixed marriages *does not vary much across denominational lines.*

The 1957 census data contained information for the whole population. If there had been some decline in homogeneity of denominational affiliation, one would expect to find evidence of it among the young and the better educated. Furthermore, one

TABLE 12
DENOMINATIONAL INTERMARRIAGE
(Percent)

Denominational Intermarriage	Catholic	Baptist	Lutheran	Method- ist	Presby- terian	Jew
Proportion of U.S. population married to member of same denomination in 1957	88	83	81	81	81	94
Proportion of 1961 alumni married to member of same denomination in 1968	86 (1,130)	84 (355)	83 (354)	86 (712)	78 (402)	97 (353)
Proportion of alumni in which marriage took place between two people whose original denomination was the same and who currently belong to that denomination	75	35	34	30	15	94
Proportion of alumni whose original denomination has remained unchanged and whose spouse has converted to that denomination	11	14	22	16	15	2

would expect that the data gathered after 1957 would show such a change.

In 1968, eleven years after the national census of religion, NORC collected data on original and present religious denominations of both the respondent and spouse, as part of its ongoing study of June 1961, college graduates. The second row in Table 12 shows the proportions of the major denominations who are presently married to spouses who share the same religious affiliation. There is virtually no difference between the endogamy ratios for young college alumni in 1968 and the general population in 1957. The tendency to seek denominational homogeneity in marriage does not seem to have weakened in the slightest.

The first two rows in the table represent data indicating present denominational affiliation of both respondent and spouse, but they do not tell us whether the denominational homogeneity in marriage has been attained by marrying within one's own denomination, or by substantial conversions at the time of marriage (or at least in relation to the marriage). However, the third row in Table 12 shows the proportion of respondents who married a spouse whose original religious denomination was the same as their own, and both of whom are now practicing that religion. It becomes clear that denominational homogeneity is maintained by Catholics and Jews through the process of marrying within one's own denominational boundaries, whereas it is maintained by other religious groups largely through considerable shifting of denominational affiliations. For Catholics and Jews it is important that one marry within one's own denomination (and far more important for Jews than for Catholics). When Catholics marry into other denominations, the non-Catholic is likely to convert. Protestants may marry across denominational lines, but then denominational change occurs in order to maintain religious homogeneity in the family.

It also appears from the fourth row in Table 12 that those of Lutheran background are able to attract a considerable proportion of their non-Lutheran spouses to join their own Lutheran denomination; thus one-fifth of the Lutherans have married people who have converted to Lutheranism, but none of the other three major Protestant denominations seems to have any special relative strength in the game of denominational musical chairs that is required to maintain family religious homogeneity.

We do not know, of course, whether the patterns of denominational change to maintain homogeneity observed in the college population are the same as the patterns in the general population, since the 1957 census did not provide information about original denominational affiliation. Further research on the subject is clearly indicated. In any case, America is still very much a denominational society since denominational homogeneity in marriage exists for at least three-quarters of the major religious denominations.[3]

The inclination toward denominational homogeneity may be rooted in the American belief that religious differences between husband and wife are not good either for the marriage relationship or for the children. This belief is probably reinforced by the fact that it is simpler and more convenient for everyone in a family to belong to the same denomination. For example, one need not worry about two sets of contributions to the support of one's church. Whether the maintenance of high levels of denominational homogeneity in marriage has any specifically religious or doctrinal significance may be open to question. Nevertheless, it is still extremely important in American society that one's spouse be of the same religious denomination as oneself.

The most careful work done on ethnic intermarriage is the soon to be published doctoral dissertation of Professor Harold Abramson.[4] Working with the 1963 NORC study of the effects of Catholic education, Abramson observes that among the parents of the respondents of the study, 80 percent were in ethnic endogamous marriages running from a high of 96 percent of Spanish-speaking Catholics to a low of 65 percent for Irish Catholics. Among the present generation, the proportion of endogamous marriages has declined to 55 percent, running from 86 percent for the Spanish-speaking to 43 percent for the Irish.[5] Two observations must be made about Table 13. First of all, even in the present generation, better than two-fifths of the original immigrant groups (German and Irish) have still chosen to marry within the same ethnic background. Secondly, the rate of ethnic endogamy declines considerably across generational lines.

TABLE 13
PERCENTAGE CHANGE IN ETHNIC ENDOGAMY
FOR CATHOLIC ETHNIC GROUPS, FROM PARENTAL
TO RESPONDENT'S GENERATION

Ethnicity of father	Percentage parental endogamy	Percentage respondent's endogamy	Difference
Spanish-speaking	96	88	— 8
Italian	93	66	—27
Lithuanian	93	50	—43
Polish	89	50	—39
Eastern European	86	39	—47
French-Canadian	79	68	—11
German	73	45	—28
Irish	65	43	—22
English	27	12	—15
Total	80	55	—25

However—and this point is extremely important—the choice of a spouse from another ethnic group is not random. When the Irish marry outside their own group, they will in all likelihood marry Germans or English (which probably means Protestants who have converted to Catholicism). When the Poles inter-marry, they are most likely to intermarry with Germans·or Italians. The Germans, when they cross ethnic lines, overchoose the Irish, and the Italians seem to find spouses of either German or Irish background the most attractive if they engage in ethnic ex-ogamy. The Irish and the Polish are inclined to have little to do with one another.

The rate of exogamy increases among the young. Thus, of Abramson's Catholic respondents, 45 percent of those in their twenties are married within their own ethnic group as opposed to 65 percent of those in their fifties. However—and this may be extremely important for predicting the future of ethnic relation-ships in American society—the Irish, the most acculturated of the Catholic groups, actually are less likely to marry out of their group if they are under forty (55 percent) than if they are over forty (59 percent). The four percentage points difference is not important. What is important is the apparent leveling off of the rate of ethnic intermarriage. Similarly, the exogamy rate for those Irish who have graduated from high school (55 percent) is somewhat lower than it is for those who have not graduated from high school (63 percent). Abramson quite plausibly suggests that this may be a function of higher levels of Catholic schooling for the younger and better-educated Irish.

One of Abramson's more fascinating findings is that marrying outside of the ethnic group is correlated with a lower level of religious commitment for both Irish and French-Canadian Catholics. If an Irishman or French Canadian marries another Catholic of a different ethnic background, his level of religiousness is likely to be lower than that of a member of his ethnic group who marries within that ethnic group. For the Germans and the Poles there seems to be little correlation between exogamy and change in religious behavior. And for the Italians, marrying a member of another Catholic ethnic group correlates with an increased level of religious involvement.

The explanation is a subtle one. The French and the Irish are the most devout of the five Catholic ethnic groups in Abramson's study. For them to marry a spouse of another ethnic group means in all likelihood to marry someone whose religious involvement is somewhat less than that which he learned in his family background. The German and Poles, who stand in the middle range of religious involvement, are not likely to encounter a spouse from a more devout family background, particularly since Poles are strongly disinclined to marry the Irish. Finally, the Italians, coming from the Catholic tradition which places the least amount of emphasis on regular religious devotion, will, if they marry out of their own group, most likely find a spouse with higher standards of religious behavior than those in which the Italian partner of the marriage was raised. In other words, the extent to which the ethnic intermarriage has an impact on religious behavior is a function both of the tradition from which a spouse has come and of the tradition from which the marriage partner has come.

From Abramson's data it is easy to conclude that with so much intermarriage going on, ethnic groups are going to disap-

TABLE 14
PERCENT DISTRIBUTION OF CATHOLIC ETHNIC GROUPS, BY ETHNIC MARRIAGE CHOICE FOR RESPONDENT'S GENERATION
(Respondent's Father by Spouse's Father)

Ethnicity of Father	Span	Ital	Lith	Poli	East	Fren	Germ	Iris	Engl	Total	
					Ethnicity of Spouse's Father						
Spanish-speaking	88	2	.	1	2	1	1	2	2	99[a]	(88)
Italian	1	66	1	3	3	2	10	10	4	100	(256)
Lithuanian	.	11	50	11	8	3	8	5	5	101[a]	(38)
Polish	2	10	2	50	8	4	17	5	1	99[a]	(135)
Eastern European	1	13	1	11	39	3	13	11	8	100	(90)
French-Canadian	1	3	1	3	2	68	9	10	3	100	(112)
German	1	4	.	10	7	3	45	20	11	101[a]	(165)
Irish	1	9	1	4	3	8	16	43	15	100	(179)
English	.	12	.	8	15	12	12	30	12	101[a]	(27)
Total	8	21	3	11	7	10	16	16	7	99[a]	(1,090)

	N	1,090
	Not Married	190
	Non-Catholic Spouses	175
	NAP Ethnicity	120
	Total	1,575

[a] Total differs from 100 percent because of rounding.

pear from American society. Abramson himself rejects such a conclusion and careful consideration of his data indicates he does so with good reason. Even if the rate of decline in ethnic endogamy from the immigrant generation to the next generation should continue among subsequent generations, it would require a substantial amount of time for the ethnic factor to cease to be an important one in the choice of one's spouse. Secondly, the tapering off of the exogamy rate among the Irish suggests that the ethnic factor may still be important for generations to come.

Thirdly, while it is perfectly true that if 50 percent of every generation marries beyond its own ethnic group, the "purity" of blood lines will become increasingly confused in generations to come, it does not follow that the ethnic groups will disappear because it does not follow that the children of ethnic intermarriages will think of themselves as hybrids. No one really knows the extent of the "decision-making" which goes on among the children of ethnic intermarriages. Whether they "choose" one ethnic group or the other, or whether they simply consider ethnicity no longer an important variable, certainly there is ample impressionistic evidence that the children of Jewish-gentile intermarriages frequently make such choices; even if explicit choice does not occur one is still faced with the question as to what influence the father's ethnicity and the mother's ethnicity may have in shifting the values and attitudes of the child of an ethnic intermarriage.

The research done, to date, strongly suggests that religion indeed plays an ethnic role in a heterogeneous denominational society like the United States, reinforcing and simultaneously being reinforced by nationality background. Denominational intermarriage does not seem to be increasing. Nationality intermarriage does seem to be increasing but it is far too early to assert that nationality groupings are being assimilated into larger religious groupings. The primordial ties of land ancestry and common faith continue to interact with each other in American society in ways which we do not even begin to understand.

Notes

1. *The Denominational Society* (in preparation).

2. There was apparently considerable Protestant Irish migration to the United States before 1800—some of it from the North of Ireland, which could authentically be called Scotch-Irish, but also a considerable amount from the South of Ireland where many tradesmen, partisans and merchants had converted to Protestantism during the penal times. This Celtic Protestant immigration came mainly through Philadelphia and into the South and described itself as "Irish" until the great waves of Irish Catholic immigration began after 1820. Since the Irish Catholics were not especially welcome, their Celtic Protestant brothers, to escape identification with the unwanted Irish Catholics, began to use the term Scotch-Irish from Ulster. Many of the St. Patrick's societies of revolutionary and post-revolutionary America were entirely Protestant but Celtic and not Scotch-Irish. Even now, I am told, in some of the remaining old St. Patrick's societies on the East Coast the presidency alternates between Protestants and Catholics each year (much like the country club that we describe in Chapter 8). A famous fictional example of the Celtic Protestants in the South is Scarlett O'Hara of Margaret Mitchell's *Gone with the Wind,* whose father was very much a Celt (witness the name of Tara for his manor) but also very much Protestant. For a long time, there was a methodology in American Catholicism that these Irish Protestants of the South had come to the country as Catholics, but had been "lost" to the church because of the shortage of priests. In fact, however, it now seems that they left Ireland as Protestants, and if they can be said to have been lost to the church at all, the loss took place before migration and not after.

3. Denominational homogeneity in marriage seems equally important in another denominational society, Canada. In 1967, 69 percent of the marriages which took place in Canada were between members of the same denomination, a slight dip from the 71 percent of 1957. It should be noted that this statistic represents homogeneity at time of marriage. Presumably, some post-matrimonial conversions would push the Canadian statistic even closer to the one for the United States (cf. 1968).

4. Harold J. Abramson, *The Ethnic Factor in American Catholicism: An Analysis of Inter-Ethnic Marriage and Religious Involvement,* Unpublished doctoral dissertation, The University of Chicago, (Chicago, Illinois, June, 1969).

5. *Ibid.,* pp. 58, 59, 60.

Chapter 8.
Social Turf

A number of zoologists and social scientists of whom the most famous is Konrad Lorenz have written of the "territoriality" of man. They argue that man, like most other animals, has a biological inclination to stamp out a certain amount of physical space as "his own" and to resent to the point of physical resistance any transgressions across the boundary of that territory. Some research evidence indicates that for specific individuals the boundaries of this territoriality can be determined with some accuracy. The amount of territory different individuals need seems to differ considerably; you can come closer to some than to others without violating the boundaries of their turf.

These writers make an interesting and plausible case, although any comparison of human behavior to the behavior of other animals has a certain amount of metaphor about it because of the vast complexity of human cultural and personality systems compared with the rather rudimentary nature of these systems in other animals. If there is a biological instinct which inclines us to define a certain piece of space as our own, the instinct operates together with cultural and personality dimensions that are quite different from anything to be found in other animals. Thus man's territoriality, even if it has biological roots, is also profoundly affected by his social structure and culture.

But whether the urge for one's "turf" has biological roots or not, no student of human behavior can doubt that it exists. Daniel Boone "moving out" to find more "elbow room", street gangs fighting over their own segment of the slums, border guards nervously eyeing each other across the line, the interminable petty boundary disputes between even countries that are supposedly friendly, children's definitions of which parts of a playroom are their own, personalizing of our hotel room by placing a picture on one table and a transistor radio on another—all of these are signs that we try to impress our personality on the area which we claim to be ours. The urge (whether cultural or biological or psychological) for territoriality may be greater in some than in others; indeed, in some it may even be vestigial, but it surely is part of the human condition.

Furthermore, it seems that our urge is not merely for turf but for "social turf." While the research data are thin to the point of being practically non-existent there does seem to be some reason to believe that man's turf is not only geographic but interactional. That is to say, his affiliation to his "place" includes a commitment not only to a segment of geography but also to the interaction network and the institutions which fill up that geographic space. Perhaps one of the principal reasons for the poor communication between the members of America's intellectual elite and the rest of the country is that intellectuals rarely are able to understand the concept of social turf. They do not understand why other Americans and particularly Americans of ethnic background are so committed to that segment of social turf that they call their *neighborhood*.

To a large segment of American society no explanation is necessary for the concept of neighborhood. They have spent their whole lives inside one or more, likely many different, neighborhoods. They may be hard put to define in formal terms what a neighborhood is, but they know one when they see one. They understand the difference between their neighborhood and other neighborhoods and they are astonished to find that there are people in the land who have never lived in a neighborhood and do not understand what it is. They are even more astonished to find that these same people cannot understand the need to defend one's neighborhood and that they dismiss loyalty to one's neighborhood as immoral or racist. There may well be an element of racism involved in much of the defense of one's neighborhood, though a fear of any strange outsider "who will not be like us" is probably more important than truly racial bigotry. But there is far more involved in a neighborhood and affection for it than fear or bigotry.

The failure of elite elements in the population to understand this is disturbing. I was once a participant at a meeting sponsored by a large private foundation to discuss the so-called alienation of "white ethnics." Very quickly the meeting broke into two separate factions. One faction, of which I was a member, argued that the dissatisfaction of many white ethnic elements with the present situation in American society was profoundly rooted in social, cultural and psychological factors that the rest of society only dimly understood and usually stereotyped. The other faction argued that, on the contrary, the problem was predominantly economic. If the annual growth in real income could be maintained at a rate of five percent a year and if occasional day care centers and other institutions were provided for the "white ethnic" groups, the alienation problem would quickly go away. The rest of us shook our heads in dismay and one participant observed, "It's easy to see that you've never lived in a neighborhood, you've never known what it's like to have your street, your school, your playground, your park, your church, your established pattern of friendships, your corner drugstore, threatened by invaders who you perceive as coming to take all these things away from you, to drive you and your friends out of your neighborhood." But those on the other side did not seem to know what we were talking about. After the controversy one of the members of my faction remarked to me, "Most of those men were immigrants from Europe after the Second World War. They had no territorial roots in the country they came from. They have spent the last quarter of a century living on Manhattan Island and have never really sunk roots in a territory there either. As brilliant and sophisticated as they are, they don't really understand what it is to be an immigrant to the United States, even in the way that their predecessors in their own ethnic group understood it fifty years ago. Maybe they don't believe that neighborhoods exist anymore."

Similarly, I do not think that the controversy over neighborhood schools and the busing question can really be understood unless those who, for what they think to be reasons of social morality, insist on busing can come to understand that not all opposition to it is rooted solely in bigotry. Bigotry there certainly is and also fear, some of it well grounded and some of it foolish. But the overwhelming negative reaction to busing in the

United States calls into play other emotions, one of the most important of which is strong personal identification with the school in one's own neighborhood, an identification which, be it noted, is by no means limited only to white ethnic groups.

Perhaps one of the reasons that social scientists are incapable of coping with the factor of neighborhood or social turf is that they have taken too literally the theories of "mass society" and have believed too literally that *gesellschaft* ("contractual") relationships have replaced *gemeinschaft* ("communitarian") relationships in most human reactions beyond the family level. The neighborhood should have been left behind in the peasant village where our ancestors lived in Europe; certainly it should have been relinquished when we moved out of the "old neighborhood" immigrant ghetto. Because they are so rootless and mobile themselves, most social analysts are astonished to discover that there can be upper middle-class and suburban neighborhoods (see Chapter 9). Even if they are forced to admit the neighborhood still exists, there seems to be an implicit conviction that the forces of urbanization, rationalization, bureaucratization and now computerization will slowly eliminate the neighborhood from American society. Neighborhoods were all right in William F. Whyte's *Street Corner Society*, but one can hardly expect them to be around in the year 2000.

Perhaps the reason that there is so much suspicion about the neighborhood is that its continuing existence runs contrary to important contemporary myths: the myth of "rapid social change" and the myth of "technological man." The first myth argues that because of the fantastic change in human life styles, and because of the population explosion and the various scientific revolutions of the last two hundred years, a situation has been created in which the only thing that is permanent is change itself. The second myth contends that because of the pace of change a new kind of man has evolved, a man who lives in Professor Harvey Cox's *Secular City* and is part of Professor Warren Bennis's *The Temporary Society*. Such men literally do not have permanent roots and do not need them; such men not only do not need but are incapable of creating myths; such men not only do not belong to tribes but have passed beyond the

stage where tribalism is conceivable; such men are at home—
and in Professor Bennis's view of things can even establish intimate relationships—in any part of the world and can move
from one part of the world to another with physical and psychological ease.

The basic assumption of these two myths is that a change in
technology almost inevitably generates (though perhaps with
some "culture lag") new values, new personalities, new human
needs, new patterns of basic behavior while at the same time
eliminating the values, needs, aspirations and behavior patterns
of the past. Such an assumption, however, is not an axiom but,
at best, a testable hypothesis. I am always amused, for example,
when I hear people talk today about the "sexual revolution" as
though promiscuity was absent in the past. Our society, we are
assured, is a permissive society, but I find myself wondering
"permissive" with regard to what? Permissive compared to Her-
culaneum, to the Rome of Nero, to the Versailles of Louis XIV,
to the London of the Restoration, of the Regency or even of Vic-
toria? For a sensible social analysis to take place, the analyst
must abandon the myth that his generation is the hinge of history and resist the quite modern temptation to label behavior as
"revolutionary" when it is merely part of the human condition.

The controversy about the twin myths of rapid change and
technological man is beyond the scope of this book. Nevertheless, I suspect that the reader who wants to investigate carefully
the existence of ethnic neighborhoods and even the existence of
ethnic groups will have to suspend temporarily, at least, his conviction that both these two myths are beyond challenge. If he
wishes to investigate the credibility of the two myths further he
might read Professor Victor Ferkiss' *Technological Man, the
Myth and the Reality*.[1] Professor Ferkiss states, "Technological
man, then, does not exist." Or he may want to pursue a somewhat more tribal Professor Cox, who concludes his pilgrimage
from *The Secular City* to the *Feast of Fools* with the following
observation:

Christian hope suggests that man is destined for a City. It is not
just any city, however. If we take the Gospel as well as the sym-

bols of the Book of Revelation into consideration, it is not only a City where justice is abolished and there is no more crying, it is a City in which a delightful wedding feast is in progress where laughter rings out, the dance has just begun, and the best wine is still to be served.[2]

Or he might listen to Professor Langdon Gilkey observe in his *Naming the Whirlwind* [3] that the basic religious needs and inclinations of modern "secular" man are no different from those of ancient man. Or, finally, he might wish to investigate Professor Clifford Geertz's *Islam Observed* [4] or the present writer's *Religion in the Year 2000* [5] to see what some social scientists have to say about whether man is secular or not.

Short of that investigation the reader must accept as a tentative hypothesis the notion that while there are some secular and technological men living in a temporary society, moving about the planet with the same ease their ancestors moved about the village (even though their biological systems revolt in the form of "jet lag"), these men are relatively few in number and do not necessarily represent the wave of the future.[6] Considerable numbers of human beings continue to live in neighborhoods and continue to be deeply attached to their social turf, to view the geography and the interaction network of their local communities as an extension of themselves and to take any threat to the neighborhood as a threat to the very core of their being. When neighborhood loyalty, already something quite primordial, is reinforced by a common religion and a sense of common ethnic origins, the commitment to the neighborhood can become fierce and passionate indeed. Its streets, its markets, its meeting places, its friendships, its accepted patterns of behavior, its customs, its divisions, even its factional feuds provide a context for life that many of its citizens are most reluctant to give up. It is curious that in a world in which the "quest for community" has become so conscious, so explicit and so intense there is such little awareness of the existence of such primordial community ties. It would be an exaggeration to say that the "urban villages" which many neighborhoods seem to be are exactly the same as the peasant communes in the eighteenth and nineteenth centuries or the medieval manors or the Teutonic tribes (or the Celtic clans) or even the Neolithic communities along the river banks of southern France. Obviously many things have changed. The social control of the neighborhood, while frequently strong, is not nearly so strong as that of the communities of the past. There are more options available, more variety to be experienced, more opportunities to leave the community permanently or temporarily, and more intimate relationships with people beyond the boundaries of the community. Work, amusement, frequently education and sometimes even worship, take place elsewhere and yet anyone who has lived in a neighborhood knows how powerful and even seductive its attractions can be.

I do not wish to canonize neighborhoods. I do not wish to argue that the instinct for social turf is always benign. Having lived most of my life in various neighborhoods, I can easily resist any temptation to romanticize them. Both the University of Chicago ethnic neighborhood called Hyde Park and the South Side Irish ethnic neighborhood called Beverly Hills can be narrow, provincial, repressive places. Like all ethnics, the inhabitants of these two neighborhoods can be so concerned about their own welfare as to ignore the needs and aspirations of others. The preservation of a neighborhood, while strongly rooted in the human condition, is not an absolute value. My principal point, however, is not that social turf is always benign or that neighborhoods represent the ultimate in human values. My point is rather that one will simply not understand ethnic groups unless one knows that neighborhoods are the places in which they live, places to which many of their members are passionately committed. Any attempt to analyze American urban society, much less to reform it, which is not based on a prior attempt to understand, from the "inside," the part that a neighborhood plays in the lives of many people is doomed to frustration.

Notes

1. Victor Ferkiss, *Technological Man, the Myth and the Reality* (New York: George Braziller, 1969).

2. Harvey Cox, *Feast of Fools* (Cambridge: Harvard University Press, 1969).

3. Langdon Gilkey, *Naming the Whirlwind* (Indianapolis: Bobbs Merrill, 1969).

4. Clifford Geertz, *Islam Observed* (New Haven: Yale University Press, 1969).

5. A. M. Greeley, *Religion in the Year 2,000* (New York: Sheed and Ward, 1969).

6. I discuss the "new tribalism" or the "new ethnicity" in Chapter 12.

Chapter 9.
One Neighborhood

The ideas that I have expressed in this volume may seem to be dangerously "un-American"; the quasi-official myth says that such bizarre, "old-fashioned" things as religion and nationality should not keep men separate. My arguments that religion and nationality offer rich cultural resources and strong cultural supports for a society seem suspicious. The assumption that "everybody's going to be like us" is rooted in the more implicit assumption that it is unsatisfactory for others not to be like us, and that with education and the passage of time they will in fact become more enlightened and be like us.

The dark and obscure tendencies of religion and nationality may flourish in the immigrant ghetto, among the working class, and the middle class, but surely among the well-educated and the well-to-do, "nice people don't do that sort of thing."

However, despite the fears expressed by many Jewish agencies, it does not seem to me that American Jews have become any less Jewish because they have been successful in American society. They, of course, have become well-educated and affluent Americans but in a very Jewish style. The New England Unitarian who modestly views himself as the standard for Americanization will wait a long time before any Jews become like him—even if a few of them become Unitarians or Ethical Culturists. Similarly, the Irish Catholic would be well advised not to hold his breath before the Italians become as religiously somber as the Irish even if they are going to parochial schools in increasing numbers. The data we presented in Chapter 6 about the persistence of ethnic differences, even among young college graduates, however fragmentary the data may be, provide no comfort for those who think that affluence and education are going to win them away from the traditions of family, religion, neighborhood and nationality, particularly when those traditions seem to be an extraordinarily useful way of finding a place for oneself in American society.

Nonetheless, the mythology would still lead us to expect that if one could find a well-to-do suburban community in which, let us say, Irish Catholics (with an intermingling of German) and Anglo-Saxon Protestants coexisted in about equal proportions, one would find little trace of religioethnic diversity. By a fortunate set of circumstances (though at times I must confess to being ambivalent as to how fortunate these circumstances really were), I had an opportunity to study such a suburban community, if not as a participant observer, at least as a participant who observed for a decade. The conclusion of my decade of observation of the neighborhood (and it truly was a neighborhood) was that the neighborhood was composed of two "invisible" ghettos. People dressed alike, earned the same kind of income, lived in the same homes, rode the same commuter trains, but occupied two very different worlds.

The Neighborhood

At first glance "Westwood" [1] might appear to be the place where the open ghetto would be least likely to appear. Located just inside the city limits of Lakeport, Westwood, unlike most suburbs, has a long history as an exclusive residential neighborhood. The earliest construction within Upper Westwood (which is coterminous with St. Praxides Roman Catholic parish) dates back to the turn of the century. Fully half of the area was built up by 1930 and most of the additional home construction was completed before 1950. Average home values in the 1950 census were over $25,000. Only three census tracts of the 1,000 tracts in the Lakeport metropolitan region had a median income higher than Westwood's $8,000 and none topped its 12.6 years median education level. Its citizens are middle-aged business and professional men who pay the highest taxes in all of Lakeport for the privilege of living on the shady, curving streets of Westwood and enjoying the vista of impeccably landscaped Georgian, Dutch Colonial and contemporary homes. As one might well expect, Westwood is a conservative neighborhood. In the 1952 election it went for Eisenhower four to one and, despite the large number of Catholics in the community, Kennedy lost to Nixon by a two to one margin. As one might not expect, however, the neighborhood is traditionally Democratic in local politics and has consistently sent a Democratic alderman to the City Hall. Westwood is also a worried neighborhood since it feels that its serenity is threatened by the Negro ghetto which is slowly moving towards it on three sides.

The Parish

Forty-five percent of the population of Upper Westwood is Catholic.

St. Praxides, the parish church of the community, was founded in 1936 and included not only a handful of well-to-do Catholics then living in the half-finished region of Upper Westwood, but also a tiny working class group clustered around the business district of the then insignificant suburb of Redwood Park.[2] Oral tradition has it that Catholics were not welcome in Westwood. A cross is supposed to have been burned on the front lawn of St. Luke's (the parish from which St. Praxides was cut off) in the late 1920's. Catholics were excluded from the tennis club and only a handful were admitted to the country club. A petition was circulated to prevent the pastor of St. Praxides from building the parish school in 1937.[3] These events are in the distant past now, but they are remembered at least vaguely by the parishioners of St. Praxides—and with resentment.

The parish doubled in size from its founding until 1940, declined somewhat in the early 1940's (after the loss of Redwood Park), spurted up to 1800 by the end of the war, and then added about one hundred members a year in the ensuing decade and a half. The increase from 1936 to 1945 reflects the minor construction boom of the late 1930's and early 1940's. Growth since 1950 is due to the increased size of families in the postwar baby boom and the replacement of non-Catholic families by Catholic families—especially in the older part of the neighborhood.

St. Praxides fits the image of a vigorous, active, modern Catholic parish. Somewhere between 85 and 90 percent [4] of its ad-mitted members crowd into the striking contemporary style church each Sunday morning. Over 3,000 Holy Communions are distributed each week, approximately half on Sunday and the rest at weekday masses. Four priests, twelve nuns and thirteen salaried lay people (including five lay teachers) serve the parish "plant." More than twenty projects and organizations—from a community lecture series with nationally known speakers to a parish blood bank—keep its meeting rooms going each night of the week. Its athletic teams are the terror of the Southwest Catholic Conference, and its laity are almost chauvinistically proud of their progressive parish (although, at times, they are a bit afraid that it might be too "progressive"). Its young people feel a close loyalty to the parish, which serves as a center for much of their activity (even though there is no parish high school). More than 90 percent of its children of grammar school and high school age are in Catholic schools.

Forty percent of the Catholic population live within two blocks of the church whereas only 20 percent of the total popu-lation live in the same area. This segregation does not appear to be the result of a conscious choice on one side or the other. Ac-cording to real estate men, home buyers rarely, if ever, inquire as to the religion of their neighbors. However, Catholics are es-pecially eager to buy homes near a church, as is evidenced by real estate ads in the Lakeport press, which often give the dis-tance to the nearest Catholic church. The public school is across the street from St. Praxides, yet Catholics easily win the compe-tition for homes in the vicinity.[5] The parish, then, is valued more as a community center by Catholics than the public school is by non-Catholics.

The religious intermarriage data is even more fascinating. From 1936 to 1955, about 20 percent of the marriages that took place in St. Praxides Church were religiously mixed, but be-tween 1955 and 1965 only 3 percent were religiously mixed. Thus, in a well-to-do community where the forces of accultura-tion and assimilation were presumably working vigorously, reli-gious intermarriage decreased instead of increasing. My hunch is that as the Catholic population of the area grew in size and in structural integration, opportunities for contact with non-Catholics decreased.

Recreational Companionship

Westwood Country Club, since its founding in 1908, has been known as one of the most exclusive golf clubs in the Lakeport region. Although its elegant Victorian clubhouse may lack the spaciousness of some of the newer clubs and its social life may be less frantic, its cuisine is excellent, its swimming pool is impressive and its eighteen hole golf course is probably the best in Lakeport.

The religious history of the club since its founding is shrouded in myth and legend. Indeed, there are practically no records of any kind of what happened at the club for anything but the last fifteen years. It cannot be established with certainty that Catholics were completely excluded from membership—though there were few Catholics until the 1940's and no approach to parity until the 1950's. The first Catholic president did not serve until 1945 and the next Catholic was not elected until 1956. Apparently, the present policy (though unwritten) is for Catholics and non-Catholics to alternate in office. At present, the balance between the two groups is almost exactly equal.[6] In 1965 there were one hundred sixty-eight Catholic members and one hundred sixty-three non-Catholic members. Two of the four officers and five of the nine board members were Catholic. In the women's auxiliary all four of the officers were non-Catholic but four of the eight directors were Catholic. Seven of the committee chairmen were Catholic and five were non-Catholic. Four of the seven membership committee members were non-Catholic. Of the fourteen new members admitted in the two years 1963–1965 exactly half were Catholic.

It should be noted that this balance is maintained without any conscious communication between the two groups on the subject of balance. Apparently, everyone takes it for granted that some kind of rough parity must be maintained. The club president (a Catholic) denies that there is even a tacit agreement to maintain this parity; but he will admit that two years ago he was the first Catholic ever to nominate a non-Catholic to the board of directors (and only after prior agreement with a non-Catholic to nominate a Catholic).

If one looks at the present situation and tries to piece together some idea of the past history, it is possible to argue that a succession phenomenon has gone on and that the present delicate and complex balance may represent a transition state. It seems reasonable to suspect that Catholics were a distinct minority in the club until 1950, that the big surge in Catholic membership came between the end of the Second World War and 1955, that the parity situation has existed for the last ten years since both groups have found it in their temporary interest to maintain parity. The remaining Protestants do not want to give up [their] club without a battle and the Catholics do not especially want to see them go since their departure will force the club to dip lower down in the Catholic ethnic pool for new members whose money will be necessary to keep the club running (which, of course, is the very reason why Catholics were admitted in the first place). How long this situation will last is problematic. A highly significant indicator of future trends is the fact that only twenty-six non-Catholic families from Upper Westwood are still members. One would very much like to know how many non-Catholics from Upper Westwood have let their memberships lapse in the last decade but, unfortunately, such information is not available.

In any case, the present situation is one in which the invisible walls of the ghetto cut across the fairways of Westwood Country Club instead of being coterminous with its fences. Depending on whom one is talking to, one can get varied pictures of the amount of fraternizing at the club's social affairs. Everyone agrees, however, that there is no segregation on the golf course.[7] However, the starting sheets from July, 1950, indicate a different picture. Two thousand four hundred eight games of golf were played during the month, 1,293 by Catholics and 1,115 by non-Catholics. Catholics from St. Praxides played in three hundred twenty-four golfing groups and in only eighty-six of these did they mix with non-Catholics. Five hundred eighty-four games were played by members of St. Praxides; in the eighty-six groups in which they encountered non-Catholic golfers, almost half the Catholic golfers in mixed groups (sixty-six) were in the twenty-two foursomes where one Catholic played with three non-Catholics. The mathematics of arranging this material are complex since there are three different kinds of golf patterns (twosomes, threesomes and foursomes).[8] Table 15 gives the ratios of actual to expected (by random distribution) interaction between Catholics and non-Catholics.

It is clear from the table that in groups of three and four golfers, members of St. Praxides tend to play with each other about seven times as often as they would in a random model. As a result, their golfing with other Catholics is more or less random and they considerably underchoose non-Catholics as partners. One would expect people to play golf more with their neighbors than with non-neighbors; indeed, this is true. It is apparent that members of St. Praxides slightly overchoose their non-Catholic neighbors in comparison to non-Catholics from outside the neighborhood. However, those non-Catholics from the neighborhood are still substantially underchosen.[9]

TABLE 15
RATIOS OF DISTRIBUTION OF GOLFERS FROM ST. PRAXIDES TO THE DISTRIBUTION WHICH MIGHT HAVE OCCURRED HAD MERE CHANCE BEEN OPERATING

Twosomes			
Both from parish	With a Catholic not from the neighborhood	With a non-Catholic neighbor	With a non-Catholic not from neighborhood
3.5	.74	.2	.12
Threesomes			
All from parish	At least one Catholic not from neighborhood	At least one non-Catholic neighbor	At least one non-Catholic not from the neighborhood
7.0	.9	.3	.3
Foursomes			
7.0	.9	.5	.3

The Open Ghetto in Westwood

The data presented in the three previous sections establishes that the amount of interaction between the religious groups is very close to the sociologist's open ghetto model.

A visitor to Westwood would think at first glance that he had come upon a remarkably homogeneous neighborhood. Its citizens work at the same kind of jobs, are in frequent business contact with each other or similar people, wear the same kind of clothes, drive the same kind of cars, belong to the same clubs, vote the same way in elections, ride the same commuter trains, frequent the same vacation spots, share the same values and life goals and die of the same kinds of diseases. But, if the visitor tarried a bit, he would find that there were two distinct groups in the community. The first thing he would notice would be that the children—after kindergarten—went to different schools. Although the two schools were across the street from each other, the playgrounds very close, little contact occurred between the children in each. Their starting and finishing times were different and rarely were students from one school walking home at the same time as the students of the other school. If groups from one school should pass groups from another, there might be an occasional polite "hello" but more frequently no exchange of greetings. Indeed, it seemed that one group was unaware of the other's existence. The two playgrounds were but half a block apart, but never did the children from one group mingle with the children from the other. Members of the Catholic group would frequently play softball or touch football on the public playground, but never with teams from the public school. Two softball games could be going on at opposite diamonds without either group being aware of the other's presence, except occasionally to throw back a stray ball.

If the visitor were to probe into the infancy of these youngsters, he would learn that little children played with next door neighbors no matter which group they belonged to, but by the latency years, as if by mutual consent, such relations were terminated. He would also learn that the two groups went to separate high schools and colleges and continued to be unaware of each other's existence—except as a part of the scenery—until they had married and left the neighborhood.[10] Should the visitor be brave enough to venture into the chaos of a St. Praxides [High Club] social, he would find that among the four hundred milling noisy adolescents there was not a single member of the other group. They were not turned away; they simply never came.

If the puzzled investigator was invited to many cocktail parties, which form the mainstream of Westwood social life, he would notice that it was a rare party where a member of one group was admitted into the home of someone from the other group (unless there was a case of mixed marriage and there are only about eighty of them in Upper Westwood). He might have taken up bridge and found that it was quite possible to engage in this popular pastime for years and never sit across a table from one who was in the other group.

He could have continued his investigations to the Westwood Tennis Club and learned that while occasionally a young tennis star might take on a member of the other group, he (or she) would never choose the other as a partner in tournament doubles. He could have gone on to the country club and noted that the young people from the two groups would be clustered at the opposite ends of the pool, that there was no dancing with members of the other group at teenage dances, that at adult parties the two groups stayed on opposite sides of the room and that even on the links it was a rare foursome which contained members of both groups.

With so much evidence pointing to separatism, our researcher would have expected to find a considerable amount of social conflict between the two groups; but he would have been disappointed. In seven years the members of Upper Westwood (or at least a group of them) publicly disagreed along strictly religious lines on only one relatively minor issue. (The issue was a swimming pool for the tennis club.) At other times, the religious issue has quickly been neutralized by leaders of both factions who pointed out that there were prominent Catholics and non-Catholics on both sides.

The religious issue has always lurked in the background with the possibility of coming out into the open, but both groups seem to have a major interest in seeing that the serenity of the community is not disturbed by religious conflict. Indeed, even the existence of the religious division is often stoutly denied.

To what extent is parish activity a cause of this division? The American Catholic parish has traditionally been a social and recreational center for its people. The "national" parish which smoothed the transition from the Old World to the New was equipped to meet virtually every need of the immigrant from a credit union to a boxing ring. The clergy argued—and with good reason [11]—that without such social and recreational services the Church would "lose" the immigrants. One would have expected that with the disappearance of the immigrants and the decline of the national parish, the need for these social and recreational services would have lessened. The need may no longer be present, but the demand for them still is.[12]

It is obvious that the existence of the parish as a recreational center inhibits the amount of social interaction between Catholics and non-Catholics. On the basis of time alone, Catholics are so busy interacting with fellow parishioners that they cannot interact with non-Catholics. It is important to note, however, that the recreational and social activities of the parish are not part of a plot to keep Catholics away from non-Catholics. Such a function is very latent indeed. The clergy promote such activities because they vaguely feel that the activities are good for "parish spirit" and because the laity want the activities and because these are things which parishes have "always done." The laity in their turn want the activities because these are the things which parishes have always done (and hence "should do") and because the parish facilities are a convenient social center. No one seriously believes that in the absence of such facilities the people of St. Praxides would cease to be good Catholics.

Thus, when dissatisfaction arose with the Lakeport Park District and the city's Catholic youth athletic leagues, it was "natural" for St. Praxides to join with other suburban parishes to form the Southwest Catholic Conference. No one thought of inviting any of the non-Catholic churches in the area to join the conference; indeed, it is doubtful that they would have accepted such an invitation. The Conference continued the separation between the two groups, and perhaps heightened the separation somewhat. No one planned such a result, but tradition and structure made it practically inevitable.

It is now, then, several years since I departed from Westwood, though for weal or woe some of it will always be with me, and for weal many of its young people will always be with me. It is terribly difficult to write about a community with which one has wrestled so long and be unbiased, but isn't this as much so for the rest of social science? Ambivalency is a functional substitute for the absence of bias. There are many things wrong with such a community and yet there are many good things about it, too. The commitment of young Westwoodians to the world far beyond their neighborhood during the difficult decade of the sixties did not, I think, make them any less provincial, for, wherever they went in the world, be it Bolivia, or Mississippi or Washington, D.C., they were unmistakably and irrevocably Westwoodians. But the point is not that they were not provincial, nor much less that they were not ethnic (for they were as Irish as anyone could be in the fourth generation), but rather that the very fact of having roots in their own strange little province gave them a posture and a perspective from which they were able to make commitments to the world beyond.[13] How sustained and how creative those commitments will be is something that only the future can tell.

There are many short-term functions which the open ghetto serves for the churches in Upper Westwood. Religious mixed marriages, which both sides consider to be undesirable, are kept at a minimum. Members of neither religious group are in any danger of being "contaminated" by the other's ideas. Conflict situations, or at least the social embarrassment that would probably arise if there were more communication between the two groups, are kept at a minimum. Both sides can feel secure that they have the loyalties of their people, that their congregations are lively, bustling organizations. Both sides can be reasonably confident that they have enough strength to resist the encroachments which the other is likely to be plotting. The clergy on both sides would face many more complicating factors if the ghetto walls should vanish.

Nevertheless, many of the long-run effects of the open ghetto are almost certain to be dysfunctional—for the churches, for Westwood, and for the larger society. No one in his right mind would imagine that the differences between Catholicism and Protestantism would be resolved if there were only more communication between the two groups. On the other hand, neither religion is going to develop, even to a reasonably full extent, the potentials of its own tradition as long as it studiously pretends that the other tradition is nonexistent in a community. Nor is there a ghost of a chance that Westwood will solve the problems which the oncoming Negro ghetto is going to bring unless the two groups are willing to cooperate intensively with each other.

I have attempted to report on the situation in Upper Westwood without probing too deeply for causes, much less seeking for someone to "blame." In such a delicate and controversial problem as the relation between religious groups, the temptation to blame one side or the other is great, even for a social scientist. Since my view of Westwood is from the Catholic side, most of the emphasis has been on how Catholics do not interact with their non-Catholic neighbors. Such a perspective might give the impression that I am blaming my fellow religionists for being "ghetto minded." Such is not my intention. If Catholics do not interact with non-Catholics, neither do non-Catholics interact with Catholics. If we ask who does not interact first, we find ourselves facing the problem of the chicken and the egg.

If we go beyond the fruitless search for a scapegoat [14] and seek to find causes, we are inevitably forced to look into the operation of historical trends—an investigation which may well seem speculative by the more rigid standards of contemporary sociology. Nevertheless, on what grounds could we reasonably expect the situation to be any different? Admittedly, the Reformation occurred some four centuries ago. Yet there have been very few situations in these four centuries where Catholics and Protestants have faced each other in the same community and with relatively equal power. Some of the European countries have similar percentages of Catholics and non-Catholics, but normally the division of population is territorial, with Catholics dominant in one section and Protestants in another. A condition of direct confrontation in a framework where there are constitutional limitations on the amount of conflict permitted is comparatively rare. In addition, the United States was for more than a century a Protestant nation. Only in very recent years has the Catholic population been admitted to some kind of equal partnership. It would be surprising if either of the partners were happy with the present situation. Catholics are no longer immigrants, but the immigrant experience is still fresh in their minds. Protestants are no longer the dominant majority, but the majority experience is still fresh in their minds. It is possible to argue that, under such circumstances, the *absence* of a multiple melting pot situation would be surprising.

Perhaps Westwood is untypical. It is Irish; it is middlewestern; it is a place of numerical parity; it has a history; its Catholic population came more or less [all at once] after the war; it is composed largely of independent professionals and entrepreneurs,[15] not organization men. Only further research in the multiple melting pot hypothesis will reveal whether a change in any of these variables might substantially affect the theory.

Ecumenism

I cannot conclude my narrative of Westwood without saying something about the impact of the ecumenical movement on the neighborhood. In a way, its impact was dramatic, for now, Protestant and Catholic clergy speak to one another and, indeed, even help one another's high school students write term papers on ecumenism. However, to suggest that the sixteen churches in Westwood might some day merge into one superdenominational religion would be greeted there only with laughter. Too many people have too much of themselves invested in their local congregations to want to see these kinds of nations absorbed. After all, in such a superparish there could be only one president of a women's society, only one head usher and, alas, only one pastor.

The first ecumenical venture in Westwood began as the Vati-

can Council was drawing to a close, and the first flush of ecumenical enthusiasm was sweeping American Catholicism. St.
Praxides' lecture series decided to celebrate this event by having
a panel discussion with one Catholic and two Protestants—a
Catholic theologian, a Lutheran theologian and an Episcopalian
archdeacon.[16] The layman who was president of the lecture series (also president of the country club) was a successful stock-
broker and a dedicated ecumenist (he danced with Protestants
at the country club dances). He suggested this panel might be
an appropriate time to invite the Protestant clergy to break
bread with the Catholic clergy of the neighborhood and, thus,
ritually symbolize the end of the counterreformation. This idea
was conveyed from the layman to the pastor through the usual
channel of communication—the curates. The pastor admitted
that the idea was a good one but said if we invited the Protestant clergy then we would "have to invite their wives." Somehow this seemed to settle the issue. We returned to the layman
with the pastor's decision and he responded by saying that,
under such circumstances, he would issue the invitations to the
non-Catholic clergy *and* their wives and to us, too, for that matter. The pastor said that he was in full accord with such a compromise.

There were a number of other issues that had to be resolved,
such as whose stationery the invitation would go out on. It was
deemed inappropriate to use the parish stationery and so the
layman's brokerage firm provided the stationery announcing the
event. There was then the question of what one served Protestant clergy to drink before meals or, indeed, did one offer to
serve them anything? Would it be offensive, for example, to ask
a Methodist minister and his wife whether they would like
something to drink? (I vaguely remembered that it would not be
offensive at all to offer such a possibility to a Lutheran.) The
solution to this problem was indeed a clever one. The dinner
would not be at the broker's house but at the local country club.
We would assemble in the lobby before going in to dinner, the
bar would be open, and the waiter would come and ask the
members of the group whether they desired any liquid refresh-
ments. Thus, the Catholic clergy and the Catholic host would be

spared the embarrassment of pressing John Barleycorn on Protestant clergy. After the many weeks of discussion that led to these solutions, the invitations were written, then rewritten and revised according to the pastor's dictates, and then finally committed to the care of the United States postal service. There was no answer for a week, and then two weeks. My own suspicions were that the telephone wires, linking the various Protestant clergymen in the neighborhood, were burning up as lengthy conversations went on as to what an appropriate response would be. Finally, on one day, seven responses came in, and the next day, three more. Eight of the clergy were delighted to accept and two pleaded quite legitimate excuses. From the other six we have, until this day, heard nary a word. However, I should not be too harsh in my judgment upon them for I was sure that if they had addressed such an invitation to us before the appearance on the papal throne of John XXIII, they would not have heard from us either.

Finally, came the fateful Sunday evening. And there we were, clergy (noncelibates accompanied by their wives) and one very nervous investment banker and spouse, presiding in the lobby of the country club over Westwood's first brave efforts at ecumenism. There was an immense problem: none of us had thought about planning what to say. We stood around and engaged in very nervous small-talk (I believe the Methodist was content with a glass of Coke) till finally my junior colleague on the parish staff broke the ice: [17]

"Well, here it is in Wittenberg, and the year is 1516."

Notes

1. All proper names are fictitious.

2. Three parishes now serve Redwood Park, which burgeoned as a suburb following World War II.

3. It is dubious how serious this petition was meant to be. It was forwarded to Alderman Kelly, who was a member of the parish and who probably never got any votes from the petition's signers.

4. The statistics on religious practice in St. Praxides have been calculated

according to a procedure described in A. M. Greeley, *Some Aspects of Interaction between Members of an Upper Middle-Class Roman Catholic Parish and Their Non-Catholic Neighbors.* Unpublished master's dissertation, (Chicago: University of Chicago, 1961), pp. 45–50.

5. In the square around the public school and its yard there are twenty-five homes, twenty-one of them owned by Catholics.

6. The religion of members was rated by several judges. In case of doubt, the vote of the majority of the raters was accepted. Only four or five families were doubtful, religion being a highly visible quality at the club.

7. Catholics tend to play more golf than non-Catholics but not significantly more.

8. Cf. Greeley, *op. cit.*, for a fuller discussion, p. 129.

9. I had hoped to find patterns of interaction at the country club, uncovering a "type" of person or an occupation which would figure more frequently in religious mixed golf. No such patterns emerged. Seven men—a doctor, a lawyer, a real estate man, a travel agent, a business executive and two presidents of small steel companies—accounted for two-thirds of the mixing that went on in foursomes.

10. One girl from St. Praxides summed up the attitude perfectly: "Oh, there was a non-Catholic girl who lived next door to us, but she rode horses all the time."

11. Houtart, for example, maintains that the flexibility of the national parishes was the main reason why the working class did not leave the church in America as it did in Europe. Cf. François Houtart, *Aspects Sociologiques du Catholicisme Americain* (Paris: Les Editions Ouvrières, 1957).

12. In fact, there is every reason to suspect that all the recreational and social activities in St. Praxides could be suppressed tomorrow and there would be no change in the level of religious practice in the foreseeable future (which is not to imply that the activities *should* be suppressed). Some neighboring parishes have no such activities and yet the level of religious practice is virtually the same as in St. Praxides. This raises the intriguing hypothesis, which must some day be investigated, that in the present state of American society, the level of a religious practice of a parish depends on social and economic factors and is almost totally independent of what the parish clergy may or may not do.

13. At the time of writing this chapter I have two research assistants, both from Westwood and, obviously, both Irish.

14. It seems pointless to me to say the open ghetto is a function of the Catholic school system. The ghetto seems to exist in areas where there is not a Catholic school system, New England. There would be more mixing if there were not a Catholic school system, but how much more is open to question. In any case, it seems to me that the school system is the depend-

ent variable and that to explain the multiple melting pot as being the result of the school system is to invert the causal relationship. The important question to ask would be why the American Church, alone of all churches in the Western world, has felt it necessary to build a school system which extends from kindergarten to graduate school.

15. As one young Westwoodian put it, "This place is the last stronghold of inner-directed man."

16. We had not yet become so sophisticated as to realize that you didn't call an Episcopalian archdeacon a Protestant.

17. Now, ironically enough, a nationally famous ecumenical theologian.

Chapter 10.
Intellectuals as an Ethnic Group

"It is the custom for intellectuals to write biographies of politicians. They generally criticize politicians for lacking the skills which are appropriate to intellectuals. One wonders what would happen if politicians should write biographies of intellectuals."

Professor Arthur Mann

America's intellectual elite, normally secure from criticism, has been taking some lumps lately—and not just from Spiro Agnew. Writing in *The Nation*, John McDermott has accused lower-level members of the elite of thinking of themselves as missionaries bringing culture to the heathens, and Michael Lerner, in *The American Scholar*, anticipated Agnew with the suggestion that the intellectual leaders may be snobs. Culture is indeed missionaried at some of the working-class institutions (state colleges are what I have in mind) at which exiled members of this elite are forced to teach to earn their daily bread, and snobbery is as present among this elite as among other groups of human beings.

I would like to suggest a way to understand the split which columnist Joseph Kraft has called "the most dangerous in American society—that between better-educated America and middle America." I propose that we can best judge the relationship between the intellectual elite and the rest of society if we perceive that the intelligentsia is, in fact, an ethnic group. Once we accept this, we begin to see the present tension between this ethnic group and other ethnic groups in its proper perspective.

There are six characteristics which delineate an ethnic group:

(1) A presumed consciousness of kind rooted in a sense of common origin.

(2) Sufficient territorial concentration to make it possible for members of the group to interact with each other most of the

time and to reduce to a minimum interaction with members of other ethnic groups.

(3) A sharing of ideals and values by members of the ethnic group.

(4) Strong moralistic fervor for such ideals and values, combined with a sense of being persecuted by those who do not share them and hence are not members of the ethnic group.

(5) Distrust of those who are outside the ethnic group, combined with massive ignorance of them.

(6) Finally, a strong tendency in members of an ethnic group to view themselves and their circle as the whole of reality, or at least the whole of reality that matters. Thus, many primitive tribes use the same word for "human being" as they do for members of the tribe. Those who are outside the group, even if they are conceded some sort of human status, are, nonetheless, not considered terribly important.

Few probably will disagree that the first two characteristics apply to members of the American intellectual elite. Although the common origin of these elitists is not based on common biological ancestors, they are still united by a powerful "consciousness of kind." Their spiritual ancestors are the same, they have attended the same universities, and they know one another rather well—through personal contact at the upper levels of the group and through reading the approved journals at the lower levels. Further, they are highly concentrated in certain ethnic enclaves—in New York, Washington, Boston, Hyde Park in Chicago, the San Francisco area. The University of Chicago scholar, for example, who has attended the Laboratory School, the college and a graduate department at the university and now serves on its faculty, is not likely to leave Hyde Park any more frequently than would a member of a Polish ethnic group leave the Northwest Side of Chicago. And when he does leave, it is to go to similar enclaves where he will be just as effectively isolated from other ethnic groups.

I will content myself, then, with discussing the application of the final four characteristics. First, however, it is necessary to try to define "intellectual elite." It is as hard to arrive at a definition of this elite as of any other ethnic group. Some men and women are clearly a part of it—the editorial staffs of the ethnic journals, the faculties of five or six major universities, the most influential commentators of the mass media—but the boundaries of the group are vague and permeable. Who is "in" and who is "out" of the group are matters for controversy. (One is reminded of the debate in Israel about how to define a Jew.) Perhaps one could say that a member of the intellectual ethnic group can be identified by the journals he reads. Subscriptions to any two of the following are sufficient to guarantee one membership at least on the margins of this ethnic group: *The New York Times, Commentary, Partisan Review, Saturday Review, The New York Review of Books, The Atlantic* (but not *Harper's*), *Dissent, The New Republic* and *The Nation*. In cases of doubt, a subscription to *The New York Review of Books* alone will suffice.[1]

Members of this ethnic group, like all ethnics, are conscious of great differences within their group and are astonished to discover that those on the outside seem quite unaware of these. Thus, the intellectual ethnics are horrified to be told that from the outside Rennie Davis, Irving Howe, Arthur Schlesinger and Joseph Alsop seem to have far more in common with one another than they do with anyone who is not an intellectual ethnic. All one can do in response to their astonishment is to ask whether they know about the deep and basic differences that separate the Polish National Alliance and the Polish Roman Catholic Union. Members of other ethnic groups will forever be convinced that a Harvard man, no matter how fierce his revolutionary rhetoric, how wild his beard, how bizarre his dress, is still at root a Harvard man. If it is legitimate to use Pole (or Irish or Italian or Jew or Swede or Chinese) as a general category without adverting to the differentiations within the group (of course, members of the intellectual ethnic group do this constantly), then there seems no real reason why those who speak of the intellectual elite (perhaps even calling it "intellectual Establishment") should be concerned with the differentiations that those inside the group consider so terribly important.[2]

First of all, we must investigate the values shared by the members of the intellectual ethnic group. The most basic value

is the conviction that the articulation of ideas is the most digni-
fied form of human activity; and closely related is the notion
that those whose role it is in society to articulate ideas are not
only the most superior members of that society, but also the
only ones really qualified to run it. It is taken for granted that
there are few problems facing society which intelligence and
goodwill could not resolve and, therefore, if problems remain, it
is because of the absence of either intelligence or goodwill on
the part of those who are responsible for governing the society.
It is taken as axiomatic, then, that the mistakes, the tragedies,
the confusions, the animosities, the unresolved conflicts, the disasters which affect the society are to be attributed either to ignorance or to malice.[3]

From there, it is one further step to see, if not a conspiracy, at
least some sort of implicitly organized plot to prevent social
progress and to frustrate the accomplishment of those intelligent
programs for social progress which the intellectual ethnic group
has devised. Given the superiority of the members of the group
and the unquestioned validity of their solutions, they do not
need to be paranoid to sniff a plot. Quite the contrary, it seems
to be the only logical explanation for the fact that they have not
yet been given a chance to make society a better place by im-
plementing all of their programs. Therefore, when they rail
against "the system" or "the establishment" or "the power elites"
or "the structure," they do so with perfect conviction and sincerity, even though to one who is not a member of their ethnic
group it seems clear enough that if there is an establishment or
a power elite or a structure or a system, then the intellectuals
are the ones who run it.

So strong, indeed, is this conviction of the superiority of intelligence and the frustration of this superiority by dark forces,
that many of these ethnics do not even see the occasional con-
tradictions in their own behavior. Thus, Theodore Roszak can
rail against "the technological establishment" and advocate his
own "nontechnological counterculture" in a book mass-produced
by a very technological printing press, published by a very establishment publishing house and marketed by the most sophisticated kinds of establishment advertising techniques.

Within the context of these twin basic convictions of the superiority of intelligence and the conspiracy against it, the precise positions this ethnic group takes on specific questions may change, though rarely is this change explicitly acknowledged. However, a number of the group's more generalized positions can usually be identified:

(1) Schools are the most appropriate place to accomplish social reform.

(2) Marxism, whatever its weaknesses may or may not be, is the most effective way of creating social progress—at least outside the United States.

(3) Youth is the hope of the future and thus the intellectual ethnic group must be profoundly concerned with what is happening among the young. Note the obsession, for example, in *The New York Times Magazine* with articles on youth culture. Note also the resolute refusal to face the fact that the youthful protest movement, in its political, psychedelic, communitarian and rock-music manifestations, represents only a small minority even of the college population, to say nothing of the total population under thirty.[4]

(4) There exists somewhere a group called "the people." This group—be it noted, quite distinct from "the silent majority"—is not nearly so well-educated as the intellectuals but does share their values and can be counted on to supply the "muscle" for whatever fantasies about grass-root support the intellectual ethnic group finds itself in need of. The composition of "the people" changes; in the 1930's it was the working class, particularly trade-union members; more recently, this group has been "the blacks," "the poor" and "the Third World." The mythology of "the people" requires, of course, that all or most of the members of these particular categories be assumed to be part of "the people." However, those presently permitted into "the people" should be wary. Membership is not permanent and can be revoked whenever the evidence becomes irrefutable that substantial elements admitted to "the people" in fact do not share the values of the intellectual ethnic group. My own hunch is that the position of the blacks is quite precarious because at some time in the reasonably near future the intellectual ethnics are

going to discover that the black militants and black radicals do not speak for the overwhelming majority of the new black middle classes—or upper black working class, either, for that matter.

Like all ethnic groups, the intellectual elite realizes that to some extent it is separated from and threatened by the rest of society. It therefore becomes necessary to invest its convictions with strong moral force, both to assure allegiance to the values by those inside the group and to provide a weapon for denouncing those who are outside of it. The nineteenth century Irish-American's concern about freedom for Ireland and the twentieth century Slavic-American's commitment to the sanctity of the neighborhood are easily matched by the intellectual's conviction of the morality of his own tradition.

The strong moralism in the intellectual ethnic is reinforced by two other factors. For one, the intellectual's roots in the Puritan Protestant and Jewish messianic past would incline him toward moralism even if there were none so bold as to disagree with him. For another, convinced as he is of his superior intelligence, the intellectual has no trouble in concluding his superior moral rectitude: he is both right and righteous. One need only read through the editorials, the book reviews and the letters columns of any of the ethnic group journals to discover the absolute and unshakable conviction of the typical intellectual ethnic about his own moral righteousness. The long and by now tiresome debate between Noam Chomsky and Arthur Schlesinger is a classic example of this righteousness. Rarely, if ever, does one encounter in any of the journals the slightest hint that anyone thinks that he might not have all the information or be mistaken in his judgments or that his opponents, either inside the group or outside of it, might possibly be men of intelligence and sincerity.[5]

A classic example of the assumption of moral superiority by the intellectual ethnic was demonstrated in Stanley Kauffmann's review of the film *Patton*. He praises the producers of the film for capturing the spirit of the "age of Nixnew." According to Kauffmann, "It seems to say, 'All right, now, we've had enough of this bellyaching; war is in us and we might as well face it.

The urge to kill—hell, the enjoyment of it—is in us, so let's not kid ourselves. And at the risk of sounding corny—what's so damn wrong with a lump in the throat at the sight of the American flag?' Perfect. I saw 'Patton' in a large theater with a large audience. The very first shot is an American flag in vivid color filling the wide, wide screen. Some defiant applause. Then out steps General Patton, minute against the immense banner, and I felt the audience lunge toward him with relief. Everything was all right again, the old values were safe. Before Patton had finished his address to his new soldiers (which is the prologue to the film), profane, soldierly, paternal, tough, before the picture had really begun, it was a solid unassailable hit."

How fortunate for Stanley Kauffmann! He alone in the whole audience was able to distance himself from the huge "lunging" immoral mass which wants to kill, and indeed wants to enjoy the killing. Kauffmann, the elite ethnic reviewer, from his pinnacle of superiority, can look with disdain on the rest of the audience. How does he know that their reactions were what he described? He knows, that's all. And if you're Stanley Kauffmann you are so morally superior that you don't have to advance proof.

The intellectual is quite capable of compassion—for the poor and the black, especially, but also for drug addicts, terrorists, arsonists, rioters, Russians, Chinese, Arabs and the Vietcong. All these compassions do him great credit, but he is singularly selective in his compassion and in his willingness to understand sympathetically and defend members of other ethnic groups. He finds it difficult, if not impossible, to experience compassion or sympathy, or even understanding, for the United States of America, and particularly for its middle-class and working-class citizens—especially if they are over thirty. This is the "silent majority," the fascist mass, the white backlash and the white ethnic racist. These are the kinds of people whom *Harper's* (a journal that caters to those on the fringe of the intellectual ethnic group) has been examining with aloof and clinical wit in the quasianthropological reports of Marshall Frady and others. See how amusing these Texans or Californians or Gary Hoosiers are —how quaint, how droll, how boorish, how fascist!

One of the reasons for the contempt and disdain directed at members of other American ethnic groups is that they don't demonstrate the required amounts of guilt. They don't feel guilty for their white racism. They don't feel guilty for the massacres at Songmy. They don't feel guilty about being members of the American middle class. If they were the morally righteous people that the intellectual ethnics are, they would feel guilty when the intellectuals insist that they should feel guilty. After all, every American white person is, by definition, a white racist and, as an editorial writer in *Trans*-action recently observed, those Americans who voted for Richard Nixon are as bad as those Germans who voted for Adolf Hitler. And Judson Jerome, writing in *Change*, engages in an orgy of personal guilt feeling because he was shocked when one of his students admitted that he felt perfectly free to steal other people's property since he was no longer hung up on the "private property" bag. Heaven only knows how guilty Jerome would have felt if the student was also stealing his wife, since he was no longer hung up on the adultery bag.

It might be thought that such contempt for the middle class or the working class is a bit premature. The American electorate did resoundingly reject Barry Goldwater. American public opinion did force the deescalation of the Vietnamese war, the first time in history that a major power has been forced by public opinion to settle for something less than victory in armed combat. Further, the American public also solidly supported most of the social reforms that the elite intellectual ethnic group has promoted over the last forty years; it forced President Johnson out of office, it has paid, with only relatively minor protests, for the world commitments which previous generations of intellectual elites got it into, and it has even provided a broad consensus for racial integration (a consensus which may, despite the mythology of white backlash, persist even to the present time).[6] If the support of middle America for the intellectual ethnic group has waned in recent years, it may well be because the intellectual ethnics have tried to force down the throat of middle America social reforms (like school busing) whose effectiveness is questionable.

The intellectuals enthusiastically embraced the militant minorities of the black and youthful populations and their denunciation of middle America on the grounds that the militant minorities were "morally superior." Historians of the future may look on the 1960's as a time not when middle America deserted the intellectual ethnic group, but rather as a time when the intellectual ethnic group deliberately turned its back on its own mass population support and began a flirtation with radical groups whose ability to bring about social change was dubious, but whose moral rectitude—at least from the intellectual elite's viewpoint—was beyond question.

It must be emphasized that this is behavior that is perfectly understandable within the context of ethnic group analysis. It is almost inevitable that an ethnic group be unaware of what is happening in other ethnic groups and project into the other groups its own fears, frustrations and disappointments. American intellectuals are profoundly frustrated by the ambiguities, injustices and seemingly disastrous trends afflicting American society. Their superior intelligence and moral rectitude tell them what the correct answers to these difficulties are; the absence of a positive response from other ethnic groups leads them to a rigid and doctrinaire position not much different in style but considerably different in substance from that of Slavic homeowners who cannot understand why other Americans are offended by the fierce loyalty with which they try to protect their neighborhoods. The Slavic ethnic cannot understand the intellectual's assumption that he has the morally correct answer; and the intellectual is quite incapable of understanding the affection for social turf which is so powerful in the life of the Slavic ethnic. Neither side is able to have much compassion for the other, though, to the credit of the Slav, it may be said that at least he doesn't pretend to be compassionate.

Of course there is, within the intellectual ethnic group, plenty of room for dissent so long as it is the approved kind of dissent. Radical Abbie Hoffman's right to dissent will be vigorously defended, but not Nixon-aide Daniel Patrick Moynihan's (even though Moynihan's alleged dissent is, for the most part, made up of phrases snatched out of context). Drug-touter Timothy Leary is to be supported, but not race-I.Q. comparer Arthur Jensen.[7]

M. I. T.'s "new-politician" Noam Chomsky has the right to academic tenure, but ex-Johnson-aide W. W. Rostow has no right to return to M. I. T. Mayor Lindsay's mistakes are to be defended and sympathized with; Mayor Daley's mistakes are to be used to continue the myth that he is a monster—even though Lindsay was able to win the support of only 45 percent of the city of New York, and Daley 75 percent of the city of Chicago (including in excess of 85 percent of the blacks of that city). Every possible attempt was made by the intellectual elite to justify the mistakes of Israeli political leadership,[8] but no possible justification is seen for the moral behavior of Irish Catholic political leaders.

Like all ethnic groups, intellectuals have their own particular combat rhetoric, which may change more quickly than it does in other groups. It was only after long years that the Irish abandoned their hatred of "the dirty A.P.A.'s" (members of the American Protection Association), and Poles are probably still convinced that their biggest enemies in the United States are "Irish Catholic politicians and bishops." The currently favorite word of the intellectual ethnic group is "revolution." Even though the movements among the young and the black are in fact anything but revolutions in any sense that this word normally conveys, it is still absolutely necessary that the movements be described as "revolution"; never mind that for there to be a revolution the revolutionaries must have at least the passive support of the majority of the population; never mind that only a tiny minority of the nation supports either the student or the women's movements, and only a minority of the blacks supports the most militant kind of black protest.

Never mind that when the minority attempts to force its will on the majority, what one has is not revolution but fascism; never mind even that some of the young and more radical members of the intellectual ethnic group, confusing the slogan of revolution with tactics of revolution (logically enough from their viewpoint), hurl bombs, revolution is the word still to be used. And if other ethnic groups are offended by such rhetorical excess, it is merely proof of their moral inferiority.[9]

Finally, the members of the intellectual ethnic group, like all ethnics, are only vaguely aware of what goes on in other ethnic groups; they do not trust members of the out-groups and seldom, if ever, encounter them with any sort of serious conversation—save in taxicabs or in Stanley Kauffmann's theater. Normally speaking, it is not necessary to be concerned about what members of other ethnic groups think because "everybody" that matters is already part of one's own ethnic group.[10]

In his own way, Spiro Agnew was right when he suggested that a relatively small group of men in the mass media have immense control over the circulation of ideas in American society. Agnew was wrong on two counts, however. There is no conscious conspiracy in this control and, secondly, it has rather less impact than either the Vice President or the intellectual ethnics would like to think. There has been practically no room for dissent either in the leading ethnic journals or in the large-circulation media from the "official" account of the Chicago convention or the Chicago conspiracy trial. Most elite ethnics are convinced that "everyone" was horrified by the behavior of the Chicago police and of Judge Hoffman because *everyone they know* was horrified and because all the right journals say that we *ought* to be horrified. It turns out that the overwhelming majority of the American public approved the behavior of the police at the convention and equally approved the conviction of the Chicago Seven. These data can be dismissed as a sign of the fascism of the masses.[11]

Because they are ignorant of and unconcerned about other ethnic groups, the intellectual ethnics are confused and frightened when they detect a change of behavior among the members of other groups. Just as they betrayed ignorance of other groups by assuming that every new scheme which was alleged to improve the conditions of the poor and the blacks would be accepted by the white majority because the scheme was sanctioned by the elite as the only moral one, so they display equal ignorance in overestimating the so-called white backlash. Despite the past records of the middle majority, the intellectual alternates between paying no attention at all to it and being terrified of it. The terror is real enough, but it does not necessarily correspond to some reality which ought to generate terror. The intellectual who shivers with delight at the fantasy of a Polish storm trooper kicking in his door at four o'clock in the morning has the same contact with reality as does the Polish homeowner on the Northwest Side of Chicago who thinks that Black Panthers are lurking in his corner drugstore. Both have created terrors for their own entertainment and delight; both are completely unaware of what really is going on in other ethnic groups; both present classic examples of frightened ethnic behavior.

All of this is unfortunate, of course, because in addition to being members of one particular ethnic group, the intellectual elite are, by definition, the idea-shaping segment of the leadership of American society. For them to be alienated from the rest of society for reasons of presumed moral superiority or ignorance of what is going on in the rest of the society is a tragedy both for them and for the whole country. Curiously enough, members of the other ethnic groups have a great deal of respect for the intellectuals, though the respect is mixed with negative feelings. It would, one suspects, take relatively little in the way of sympathetic understanding on the part of the intellectual ethnics to begin to reestablish some kind of communication with the rest of America.

Notes

1. Since I am on the staff of a large elite university and read most of the above journals I would, under normal circumstances, be accorded membership in the ethnic group. But I am a dubious case since, in addition to being Irish (a highly suspect quality at best), I am also of the clergy. I think both of these characteristics would be forgiven me if I should marry (which, by the way, I have no intention of doing). Currently an Irish clergyman can make it into the ethnic group by seeking a wife, just as an Irish politician can by being assassinated.

2. Occasionally a member of the intellectual ethnic group ventures forth to a work situation where other ethnics are to be found, gets a job in such a situation for a rather brief period of time and then reports back to the members of his own group about the fascinating and bizarre behavior in which other ethnics engage—much as Marco Polo reported on China. Such reports are inevitably fascinating since they combine the joys of voyeurism with the pleasures of slumming. The writer feels that he is "telling it like it is" and the ethnic readers are reassured about their own moral and intellectual superiority. Elinor Langer's account in *The New York Review of Books* of her adventures at the New York Telephone Company is a classic example of this variety of literature. The other ethnics ("Polish, Jewish, Italian, Irish, black, Puerto Rican") are typical members of the consumer society. "Packaging is also important: the women will describe not only the thing, but also the box or wrapper it comes in" (how strange and fascinating of them!) . . . "they are especially fascinated by wigs" (just like Marco Polo's Chinese with their pigtails) . . . "The essence of wiggery is escapism" (what else?).

Miss Langer is more perceptive than most such amateur anthropologists. She realizes that she may have been dishonest with her subjects: "I have a strong feeling of bad faith to have written this at all." But, having thus candidly confessed her feelings, she frees herself and her readers from any awkward feelings of guilt and concludes with the marvelously ethnocentric message to her former coworkers: "Perhaps the intellectual and political values of my life by which I was judging yours make equally little sense. Perhaps the skills which give me leverage to do it allow me only to express alienation and not to overcome it; perhaps I should merely be thankful that I was raised an alpha and not a beta."

3. In matters of "thou shalt not kill," "thou shalt not steal" and "thou shalt not bear false witness," intellectual ethnics are as stern as their Puritan ancestors. However, most of the traditional violations of "thou shalt not commit adultery" are considered, if not praiseworthy, at least understandable, in terms of the offender's childhood. No attempt to justify political corruption, for example, in terms of the politician's childhood experience is likely to be listened to.

4. Rennie Davis will probably not dance on Judge Hoffman's grave, but there is a good chance that George Wallace will dance on Davis's—and perhaps a lot of other people's, too.

5. Chomsky is obviously at an advantage in his debate with Schlesinger, because Chomsky has never been part of the political administration as Schlesinger has, and, hence, has never had his moral purity tainted by political decision making. Yet one wonders about Chomsky's morality. If really convinced that American society is as imperialistic and demoralized as he claims, why would he continue to accept income from M.I.T., which

is about as much a part of the American establishment as an institution possibly could be?

6. One looks in vain in the history of the human race for a situation where a major power has been forced to withdraw from a war because a large segment of its people (and not simply a tiny minority of vocal demonstrators) would not support the war. One further looks in vain for a military establishment which would bring charges against senior officers (including generals) for an atrocity committed in a war, especially when that war was still going on. The intellectual ethnic group copes with this unexpected display of national morality by claiming credit for it. The other ethnics can't win: If they are moral, the intellectual ethnics assume that they are the ones who are responsible for the morality.

7. I am persuaded by the essay of Professor Arthur Stinchcombe in the *Harvard Educational Review* (1969) that Jensen's research on the biological roots of racial differences in I.Q. scores is inaccurate, but from inaccuracy it does not follow that he is a racist.

8. One of the more interesting developments within the intellectual ethnic group is increasing sympathy for the Arabs. Such sympathy is particularly fashionable among young Jewish radicals who combine support for the Arabs with justification for black anti-Semitism in the belief that Jewish merchants do indeed victimize the black poor.

9. In the last four years the rhetoric and the tactics of the New-Left wing of the intellectual ethnic group have suffered one of the most complete defeats in the history of American politics. Seventy percent of those who favored immediate withdrawal from Vietnam approved the way the Chicago police responded to the convention protest. The Vietnam moratoriums strengthened rather than weakened President Nixon's policy (and sentiment in favor of withdrawal went up from 21 to 35 percent after the New Left was driven into retreat by the silent majority talk). At most, only 10 percent of the country approves of the New Left (whose shouts of "Power to the People" indicate a very strong death urge; if the "people" had their way, most of the New Left would be behind bars), and New-Left tactics are the kiss of death for any program or candidate. Despite the abysmal failure of the New Left and its playing into the hands of those who oppose social progress, the intellectual ethnic group has not asked why the New Left failed, nor even really acknowledged that it has in fact failed, save by expressing fear of a "reaction," when a more appropriate fear would be that a New Right might use the New Left's tactics—and with far more effectiveness.

10. A good way to define an intellectual ethnic is to say that he thought that Norman Podhoretz really "made it" when he became editor of *Commentary*.

11. It is not my intention to side with the silent majority on either of

these issues. The point I wish to make, however, is that if the intellectual ethnic group were a little less concerned with its own rectitude and moral purity and a little more concerned about understanding what was going on in the United States and providing broad consensus for social change, it might begin to ask itself whether the members of other ethnic groups are saying something very important, however inelegantly, by their reaction to both the demonstration and the trial. However, it is much easier to dismiss other people as fascists than to try to understand them.

Chapter 11.
The Irish: An Ambivalent View
of One Ethnic Group from the Inside

"If a man is not loyal to his friends, he will never be loyal to an idea."

Young Irish politician, 1970

Ideally, the present volume would contain a number of chapters on different ethnic groups, attempting not so much to describe the history of each group in this country, but rather to depict their present situation. Unfortunately, I do not have the knowledge or the competency to present such essays. Furthermore, given the lack of scholars who specialize in these fields and the absence of adequate social research data, I very much doubt that at the present time anyone is capable of such a series of essays. However, since one of the principal purposes of this book is to stir up discussion, it may be sufficient to attempt a preliminary essay about one ethnic group, the one I happen to know best.

By way of illustration, therefore, I now offer an ambivalent view of the American Irish, or at least an ambivalent view of four aspects of the contemporary life of the Irish ethnic group —their politics, their self-image, their church and the next generation.

1. IRISH POLITICS: The first thing that must be said about Irish politics is that despite the overwhelming assumption to the contrary, the research evidence seems to indicate conclusively that the Irish are one of the most liberal of American ethnic groups, more liberal on most issues than the Scandinavians and almost as liberal as the Jews. (The data that support this statement are presented in Chapter 6 and in the Appendix.) There are two reasons why many Americans, including, be it noted, the most self-critical of the Irish Americans, have impressions that run

strongly against the data. First of all, the principal contacts between the Irish ethnic group and the intellectual ethnic group are in Boston and New York where the Irish communities for historical reasons tend to be closed and suspicious of other ethnic groups, especially if these other groups happen to be identified with what the Irish take to be the hostile WASP aristocracy. In both these cities, the Protestant and, to some extent, the Jewish ethnic groups—as well as the intellectual ethnic group —have historically been in competition with the Irish for power. Since all three of these groups consider themselves by definition to be enlightened and progressive and since their control of the media has enabled them to convince themselves of their enlightenment and progressiveness, it follows necessarily that any group that contends with them for power must be benighted and reactionary.

I would not want to argue that the Irish of Boston and New York are a singularly enlightened lot. On the other hand, when we realize that in the "establishment" press of the nineteenth century a stereo typical cartoon figure of Paddy was an ape, we find that the Irish had some reason for thinking of "establishment" groups as hostile and unwilling to sympathetically understand the Irish perspective.

But there is a more serious reason why Protestants and Jews, and particularly their more intellectually elite members, are suspicious of the liberalism of the Irish. It is a very different kind of liberalism. Edwin Levine, in his book *The Irish and Irish Politicians*, points out that the Irish politician is a nonideological man, choosing to play the role of the pragmatic broker of power and to accomplish his social change well within the framework of consensus that such power brokerage makes possible. The cement by which he binds together his political organization is not common ideological commitment but personal loyalty. He does not enjoy the trappings or prerogatives of power but merely its exercise and is frequently content to play a behind the scenes role in the game so long as he can play in the game. Given his pragmatic orientation, the Irish political leader is not terribly concerned about moral purity—save in matters of sex. Government is seen as a complex, delicate, balancing act in which one must be sensitive to the faults and frailties of men. As long as a politician is loyal to his friends and does not desert his wife and family, other evils may be tolerated as being an elemental part of the human condition. Given the strong good-government orientation of Protestants and Jews, this tolerant element of the Irish style seems corrupt and immoral. But the Irish political leader shrugs his shoulders in response and says that at least he is able to get things done and the good-government people usually are not.

Another aspect of the Irish political style has been described by Professor James Q. Wilson in his study of the behavior of Irish police, which I mentioned previously. He discovered that given a choice of a formal bureaucratic mode of communication and an informal, unofficial and indirect method of communication, Irish police sergeants almost invariably choose the latter, while sergeants of other ethnic groups tend to choose the former. The Irish sergeant—characteristic, I would say, of most Irish who engage in the political game—prefers the subtle hint, the wink of the eye, the ambiguous sentence, and the delicate innuendo, to the direct order. He prefers to work on the margins of the system rather than through its clearly established channels. He prefers the flexibility that comes with ambiguity rather than the rigidity which he feels comes with clarity.

Both Wilson and Levine see explanations for this behavior in the Irish past. During the penal, post-penal and prerevolutionary times in Ireland the political system was hostile to the Irish Catholic who had to live with it whether he liked it or not. Survival and success depended on skills that were necessary to get around the system without seeming to violate it. In the Ireland of the eighteenth and nineteenth century there was little or no room for ideology and the formal regulations of the system were hostile and punitive. The Irish therefore became masters at operating on the margins and in the interstices, saying one thing and doing something slightly different, agreeing with their lords and deceiving them behind their backs, apparently accepting the law but using the weaknesses and ambiguities of the law to triumph over those who had made and enforced the law.

Visitors to contemporary Ireland are astonished at the Irish characteristic of responding to one question with another. One friend of mine, for example, claims that he never heard a declarative sentence in his whole two weeks in the land of his ancestors. He cites as a classical example of this his experience in an attempt to ask where the post office was. "Is it a stamp you want to buy?" responded the native—even though in fact the two of them were standing in front of the post office.

Levine suggests that the Irish political style has also been profoundly affected by the governmental style of the Catholic church. There can be no doubt that the informal, indirect, nonideological approach of the Irish ward committeeman or precinct captain does bear a certain similarity to the operations of the Roman curia though my own particular biases would suggest that the precinct captain and the ward committeeman have proved far more nimble in keeping up with social change than have the curialists. However, the traditions have different origins; the Irish, despite their loyalties to the Pope, have always had a profound distrust of the curia. There is no reason to deny that Irish ecclesiastical politicians are rather like their civil counterparts, but my own inclination is to think that the two are influenced by a common cultural background and that, if anything, the churchmen learn from the civil leaders; by and large, the civil leadership is far more effective at the political style than the ecclesiastical leadership or at least quicker on its feet.

A further aspect of the Irish political style is its desire to win. Its pragmatic roots in the penal past seem to have left the Irish style not only without a taste for ideology, but also without the ability to enjoy illusions. The Irishman wants to win so badly that he can taste it, so badly, in some instances, that he will stop at almost nothing in order that he might win. He might justify himself by saying that his ancestors had few victories in the past (though a critic would respond by saying one of the reasons they had so few victories is that they were not able to stop fighting themselves for sufficiently long periods of time to fight their common enemies). For him, a politics not oriented toward victory is a vain and foolish politics. Most of the young well-to-do liberal Irish unhesitatingly jumped on the Robert Kennedy bandwagon in the 1968 campaign. They were quite baffled by the behavior of their age peers in Senator McCarthy's "magical mystery tour." For, as the young Irish Americans constantly repeated to me, "He can't win!" That winning might be less important than assuming an ideologically pure or morally correct position was something that my young friends found completely inconceivable.

2. SELF-ESTEEM AND THE IRISH: The mythology about the Celt is contradictory. He is thought of as the happy-go-lucky, playful comedian singing Clancy Brothers songs and "heisting" a few on St. Patrick's day. But he is also thought of as the moody, melancholy William Butler Yeats, seen in the mists arising from the peat bog. The statistical data are contradictory, too. On most measures of emotional well-being the Irish score higher than many other American ethnic groups. On the other hand, the fascinating research on hospital behavior suggests that the Irish repress even the acknowledgement of pain or symptoms while other groups, such as the Italians, if anything, exaggerate their reaction to suffering in hospital situations.

The whole question of personality and society is one that is far beyond the scope of the present volume. Obviously, many Irishmen have no trace of the leprechaun in their personality and still others manifest no part of the banshee syndrome. Nevertheless, there is a strong impression that there is something rather unique in Irish family life which does produce a strain of self-hatred which, while it may be different from Jewish self-hatred (there are no Irish Portnoys, not yet, anyhow), nonetheless is fairly common in the American Irish experience. The alcoholism data offer overwhelming evidence that there is something peculiar going on in the Irish family and personality structure. The Irish are twenty-five times more likely than the typical American to suffer from alcoholism (though, for whatever consolation it may bring, they are apparently somewhat less likely to be alcoholics than are Mormons).

Having dealt with the Irish in one capacity or another for most of my life, I feel on sound ground when I say that they have a powerful self-esteem problem rooted in the coldness, not to say harshness, of Irish familial relationships. If the Jewish mother, at least in the stereotype, controls her children by smothering them with affection, the Irish mother tends to control them by withholding affection. The characteristic Irish alcoholic syndrome is of the compulsive perfectionist who feels that he has never been loved for who he is but only for what he can do (the syndrome is especially prevalent in the Irish clergy).[1]

I am not asserting that no affection is felt between husband and wife, between parent and child—particularly between mother and son—in the Irish family, but I am saying that there is a strong tendency to conceal affection. The domineering Irish mother, surrounded by bachelors and old maids, is far too common a figure in reality as well as in fiction to be lightly dismissed.[2] I suspect that the large number of "vocations" to the priestly and religious life found among the Irish can in part be attributed to the fact that the Irish mother does not lose her priest son or her nun daughter to anyone else. Again, the light-hearted Irish wake so well known in fiction and the stony-hearted Irish wake which abounds in fact if not in fiction are manifestations of a personality which has not learned how either to celebrate or to mourn.

This repression of affect—save for an occasional release under the influence of John Barleycorn—may be in part attributed to religious faith though surely other national manifestations of Roman Catholicism take very different emotional forms. Cultural, historical and child-rearing practices are, I suspect, far more important than religious faith, though the frequently Jansenistic style of Irish Catholicism unquestionably rationalizes, reinforces and justifies the suspicion of emotion and affect which seems to be part of, if not the Irish personality, at least the personalities of many Irishmen.

In Chapter 6 I presented data that seems to indicate that the Irish are less likely than most ethnic groups to interact with their parents and more likely than most ethnic groups to interact with their siblings. My hunch is that this is a manifestation of the alliance that Irish brothers and sisters frequently form, both to support their parents (especially their mother) and also to defend themselves against the parents (especially their mother). *House of Gold* presents a brilliant description of how an Irish family rallies around their dying mother to support her

in her death agony—a death agony which need never have occurred if the family had provided her with the proper medical
care.

Some observers see a relationship between this lack of affect
among the Irish and the Irish method of birth control; in the old
country late marriage seems to have been until very recently the
principal means of controlling population. However, such a
form of population control is a relatively recent phenomena. In
the years before the potato famine the Irish married very young
and had large families, producing the highest birth rate in any
of the European countries. I suspect that far more is involved in
their low affect and relatively demonic view of sex than simply
a means of population control.[3] We are on very uncertain
ground in these speculations. Impressions, little bits of data,
folklore (like the old saying that the Irish are great at hating but
not very good at loving) hardly are a basis for any convincing
descriptions of the relationship between child-rearing and adult
personality in a given ethnic group. They have been presented
in this chapter as interesting speculations and as possible hy-
potheses for further research.

3. THE IRISH AND THEIR CHURCH: David L. Edwards, in his
Religion and Change, points out that while social forces can
empty churches, they can also fill them; for weal or woe, the
social forces have filled the churches of Irish Catholicism. In
the old country the identification of Catholicism with Irish
nationalism—courtesy of mother England—assured Catholicism
a hold over the devotion of the people, which generations of
ecclesiastical tyranny, obscurantism and ineptitude have not
weakened in the slightest. In the United States the hostility
of the WASP establishment to the Irish Catholic immigrant
guaranteed the continuation of this identification of Irish and
Catholic, an identification which has not been notably weakened either by the pilgrimage from the immigrant slum to the
professional suburb nor by the transformation of a counter-
Reformation church to an ecumenical church. There is absolutely no sign of schism or apostasy within the American Irish
Catholic population and no reason even to think that such a
sign will be apparent any time in the present century.

In many American Catholic liberal circles it is fashionable, indeed, almost de rigueur, to decry the influence of the Irish on American Catholicism, though, as Philip Gleason has repeatedly observed, the critics are never sure which brand of ethnic Catholicism they would have preferred to have had a formative influence on the Catholic church in the United States. Members of other ethnic groups, of course, bitterly resent the disproportionate power and influence the Irish have both within the American church and as Catholic representatives beyond the church. But they have not been able to do anything about it largely, I suspect, for the same reasons that it has taken a long, long time for any of the other Catholic ethnic groups to begin to replace the Irish as the dominant figures in urban political life.

Whether this Irish dominance has been functional or dysfunctional for Catholicism in the United States, it has certainly facilitated the acculturation of the Catholic church into American styles. But it has done so at the price of antagonizing and occasionally alienating members of other Catholic ethnic groups from the church and also of inhibiting the contributions of these ethnic groups to a more pluralistic Catholicism.

Paradoxically, the radical critics, the innovators and the reformers within American Catholicism are also mostly Irish (with an intermingling of some Middlewestern Germans influenced partly by the populist tradition of the plains and partly by the social and liturgical reforms from the German church communicated to America principally through the Benedictine monasteries, and especially St. John's monastery in Collegeville, Minnesota). A look at the roster of the various editors of *Commonweal, The National Catholic* and the *National Catholic Reporter* and at the names of those clergy and laity who are most critical of American Catholicism and most likely to be the leaders of reform organizations shows that it is the Irish who are the ones most likely to be critics of Irish Catholicism.

If there is no sign of an appreciable exodus of the Irish from the American church—even though now they are truly in the final stages of the acculturation process—there are still some fascinating signs of a modification in the relationship between well-to-do Irish and their church. First of all, there has been a precipitous decline in recruitment to the priesthood and the sisterhood in the American church. What is not so generally well known is that this decline is limited almost entirely to the Irish. Other ethnic groups, the Italians and the Poles, for example, are probably contributing larger numbers of religious "vocations" than they have ever done in the past. There are a number of possible explanations for the phenomenon. The Irish may have reached that location in the acculturation process where the priesthood is no longer perceived as a means of social mobility nor even as a thoroughly responsible and respectable profession. It may also be that the Irish clergy are most likely to be affected by the present identity crisis affecting the Catholic clergy in the United States and, hence, they may be the ones most likely to refrain from recruiting other men to the priesthood. Also, the antagonism that many suburban Irish feel toward their clergy may have substantially modified the image of the priesthood in the Irish Catholic home. Finally, the indecisiveness which I observe among the younger generation of Irish Americans (about which more later in this chapter) may also make it difficult for them to engage in the permanent commitment which the priesthood and the religious life still require.

There is some statistical evidence [4] that respect for the clergy is notably decreasing among American Catholics. In 1952 Catholics had more respect for their clergy than did Protestants and Jews, whereas in 1965 they had less. My hunch is that this phenomenon is especially prevalent among Irish Catholics. Until better data and better explanations are advanced, I would hypothesize that the antagonism of the suburban Irish towards their clergy results from the professionalization of the Irish population and the nonprofessionalism of their clergy. The most frequent charge heard against the priests in suburban Catholic communities is that they are inept, untrained and bungling. A new, well-educated and successful suburban professional class is apt to be particularly rigorous in demanding professional behavior from others. Clergy are viewed, perhaps correctly, as glorified amateurs who are not particularly good at any one thing and perform inadequately most of the things they attempt to do, from financial planning to Sunday preaching. In addition, many of the suburban professionals seem very unsympathetic and even hostile towards the younger clergy in their "identity crises." As one sophisticated and quite liberal suburban matron put it, "Our young priests don't give a damn about us. We're not black, we're not poor, we're not drug addicts, we're not teenagers, we're not hippies, so we're assumed not to have any religious need. The only kind of religious activity which they seem to enjoy is denouncing us as corrupt, immoral members of the middle class." This woman's reaction is by no means atypical. The Irish are no longer willing to excuse "poor father's" problems on the grounds that however inept—or however alcoholic—he may be, he is still a priest. If my impressions are accurate, the phenomenon is extremely interesting. The professionalization of Irish suburbanites and the lack of professional skills in their clergy may have accomplished what a thousand years of British rule was unable to accomplish—turning the Irish into anticlericals.

Another phenomenon of the Irish relationship with their church is the rise of the so-called "underground." Perhaps thousands of small groups of Catholics have banded together around priests in various parts of the country to form ecclesiastical communities which, while they are not separated from the official institution of Roman Catholicism, have no proper status within it and, in fact, work quite independently of its regulations and its structures. These underground communities, almost always liturgical and frequently social action oriented, represent a revolt against the size, the machinelike "efficiency" and the theological conservatism which are said to be typical of most official parishes. The members of the underground are, for the most part, not less religious than the members of the official parishes, but more so, though they would choose to define "religious" in somewhat different fashion. The Sunday mass attendance, the residual dietary laws and the regulations of canon law are taken very lightly indeed by the underground clergy and laity alike. It is my impression—though only an impression—that the Irish are tremendously overrepresented within the underground groups, if only because the initiative and independence required to convene or become a member of an underground community probably presuppose an advanced acculturation into American society. It is too early in the history of the underground to evaluate what contributions it may make to the future of American Catholicism. The Irish have a long history of secret organizations—the Fenians, the Lamb League, the IRA and the Sinn Fein—and in the old country the clergy were frequently the leaders of such organizations. They are unquestionably the leaders of the new underground in American Catholicism.

4. THE NEXT GENERATION: Obviously the most critical question regarding the future of the Irish ethnic group in the United States is the question about where its young people are going. Having spent most of my professional life dealing closely with the younger American Irish, I have strong opinions—alas, unsupported by statistical data—on the subject. I might also say that these opinions are even more ambivalent than the other opinions presented here.

Like their parents before them, they are a pragmatic, politically oriented group inclined towards what they take to be the practical liberalism symbolized by the Kennedy clan. For them the collapse of the walls of Camelot was a special disaster and they are by no means ready to give up the conviction that Camelot can be reconstructed. For the most part, they are not dropouts, not inclined to drugs, political protest or the hippy-communitarian culture. Although they may be tempted to flirt with these responses to American society, they are much more strongly oriented towards practical reform. Research data indicate that the Irish are overrepresented in the fields of law, political science, history and the foreign service. There also is some reason to suspect that they may be overrepresented in the Peace Corps and other volunteer movements. Anyone who has dealt with them as closely as I have is fully aware that the flair, the poetic command of language which marked past generations, is still very much alive and well. But not exactly functioning.

For if I were forced to use a single word to describe the American Irish youth I know, that word would be "indecisive." Literate, sophisticated, witty, they nonetheless have yet to become political leaders, poets or storytellers. There are no younger versions of the Kennedys or of J. F. Power, Flannery O'Connor and Edwin O'Connor. It is not, I think, that the abilities do not exist, but the courage to exercise these abilities is strangely absent. The Irish have been in the United States long enough to begin to produce their own aristocracy (an aristocracy which governed the country for an all too brief period). But that aristocracy seems paralyzed when faced with the challenge of artistic and literary creativity and productivity. Something has happened in the transition from new rich to established rich that has struck at the root of the Irish self-confidence—a self-confidence which was always uneasy at best.

My own tentative explanation is that the present generation of Irish who ought to be the creative artists and creative political leaders are depression children either in the sense that they were born during the late years of the great depression or the Second World War or at least that their parents spent their own formative years during the depression crisis. Products of the lower middle class that they were, the depression Irish have experienced dizzying success in the years since 1940 but also they have been tormented by guilt feelings over their success and the fear that their children will not be adequate to the fierce competition which they assume is required for success.

The offspring of other ethnic groups may have been "spoiled" by overpermissive parents, but overpermissiveness is scarcely the problem among the Irish. While some types of permissiveness may have been honored in the Irish family, generally authoritarian child-rearing practices among the new rich Irish appear to have produced a generation notably lacking in even the rudiments of self-confidence and self-esteem and in the ability to make decisive commitments of any sort. For the young Irish American of the fourth generation to depart from the narrow goal of career achievement expected by his parents involves an emotional risk so great that few seem willing to risk it. Even though their personal tastes may run to politics or the arts or literature, their internalized value systems not only make them feel guilty when they indulge such tastes but also prevent them from committing their full talents to their pursuit.

In other words, the transition from new rich to established

rich has involved for the Irish an accentuation of their traditional problem of self-esteem. It may also mean an accentuation of the problem of alcoholism.[5] The image of the suburban professional who achieves moderate success and does indifferently well in a career which does not satisfy or challenge him is not limited to the Irish professional class. But I believe that it is probably worse among the Irish and that would be very bad indeed.

So the American Irish, politically liberal but pragmatic, evolving new forms of relationship with their church, as much frustrated as anyone else and perhaps more so by suburban life, and so far making little progress in their peculiar problems of self-rejection and low emotional affect, face the next stage of the acculturation process in American society. Most of them undoubtedly believe that the political freedom, economic abundance and physical comforts they have acquired by migrating from the land of mist and bog to the great supermarket across the seas have been well worth whatever costs they've had to pay.

Notes

1. See the article by James Gill, M.D.,S.J., "Why We See It in Priests," *Medical Insight* (December 1969), pp. 21–32.

2. For a classic description of this phenomenon, see the novel, *House of Gold,* by Elizabeth Cullinnan.

3. One of the things that struck me very forcefully in the mother country was how Irish husbands and wives, at least in the presence of others, spoke to one another through the third party. The wife would say things about the husband to the third party and then the husband would respond to the third party saying things about his wife. (The remarks were just as likely to be flattering as unflattering.) But rarely in the course of conversations would husband and wife speak directly to one another.

4. See Andrew M. Greeley, Martin Marty and Stuart Rosenberg, *What Do We Believe?* (Meredith Press, 1967).

5. A problem which incidentally the "Pioneer" movement (a total abstinence group) has now seemed to have solved in Ireland. Alcoholism in Ireland is not only lower than it is among Irish Americans, it is even lower than it is in Great Britain.

Chapter 12.
Ethnicity and Tribalism

Most of the operations of the ethnic factor described in this book have been, if not unconscious, at least implicit. One thinks of oneself as Polish because one has always been Polish. One acts as if one were a Jew because it never occurred to one that there were alternatives. One's political style is Irish because it is unthinkable that one engage in any other political style. One does not choose to be Irish or Polish or Jewish the way one would choose to play the piano or take a trip to New Guinea or study sociology. One's ethnic background, indeed, is a component of one's identity, but one does not sit down and consciously examine the merits of an ethnic component of identity, and then equally consciously set about developing such a component, surely not if one is an immigrant or the son of an immigrant or, quite possibly, the grandson of an immigrant. However, at the present time, there are a number of social trends in American society which may force us to revise much of our thinking about the role of ethnic identity in American society. I call these trends a "A New Tribalism," for there are now a number of young people who are very consciously and explicitly seeking an ethnic identity because this fits in with other values they profess and other trends of which they are a part. Should a reflective search for ethnic identity become widespread, the ethnic factor may be considerably more than just a residual variable in American society in years to come.

Many young Americans are presently in the midst of a revolt against technology, bureaucracy and science. The psychedelic world with its drugs and rock music, the communitarian movements hoping to establish a "counterculture" based on intensely intimate relationships among those with shared values, the resurgence of primitive religious forms, such as astrology, witchcraft, divination, fortune-telling and spiritualism (along with the popularity of such less primitive religious activities as contemplation and mysticism), the search for charismatic leadership, the enthusiasm for "total" relations, the manifold variations of sensitivity training—all these are an explicit and conscious attempt to transcend the rationalistic bureaucratic formalized pattern of relationships which they believe characterize mainstream American life.[1]

Thus, even excluding the various direct-action and even anarchist political movements presently popular among some young Americans, the concern about the nonrational, primordial and affective dimensions of human relationships is very strong. Marshall McLuhan is by no means the only one who sees a new tribalism emerging. I suppose this tribalism is, to some extent, an attempt to imitate the "tribalism" characteristic of certain black nationalistic movements. If it is legitimate, indeed even mandatory, for blacks to wear their hair "natural," dress in dashikis and be deeply concerned about African politics and African culture, then, similarly, it may be legitimate and even mandatory for members of other ethnic groups to be similarly concerned about their own cultural backgrounds.[2]

But while the emphasis on black culture may have reinforced tribalism, impulses in this direction probably were already so strong that even in the absence of black militancy, tribalism would still have emerged as a fascinating aspect of campus life in the United States. Undoubtedly, the new tribalists are a small minority of youth culture. However, they are the minority which tends to be the fashion setter. If the revolt against the "depersonalization and dehumanization" which the technological society is alleged to create continues, then there is every reason to think that more and more young people will be asking questions about their ethnic backgrounds as they try to fashion for themselves an identity which has strong nonrational components. Should the antitechnology trend be irreversible—and it may well be—a whole new kind of ethnicity—self-conscious and reflective—may emerge in American society. Four important indicators of such a resurgence would be worth watching:

1. AN INCREASE IN INTEREST IN THE "HIGH CULTURE" OF THE VAR-

IOUS ETHNIC TRADITIONS: Being Polish or Irish or Jewish or Italian is still very important to large numbers of Americans. But most of those who are Irish have not read Yeats or Synge, most of those who are Italian have not read Dante, and at least many of those who are Polish have not read the works of the Polish novelist Henryk Sienkiewicz. The immigrants were generally not part of the high culture, and an attempt by their descendants to come into contact with the high culture would have very little to do with any ethnic tradition that has been handed down to them, but would represent rather a self-conscious attempt to seek some sort of personal meaning within a cultural tradition which in actuality may have been partially responsible for driving their ancestors out of their country of origin.

2. VISITS TO THE SITE FROM WHICH ONE'S ANCESTORS CAME: An increasing number of young people—though I have no way of knowing how many—are fascinated by the possibility of visiting the town from which their families came or even spending a year abroad studying at a university in the ancestral nation. In neither instance are they "going home" to visit relatives they know or to reestablish relationships which were once a part of their lives. Instead, they are trying to find something out of which they can create a past for themselves.

3. AN INCREASED USE OF ETHNIC NAMES: Ethnic names appear to be growing in popularity, although young parents do not always choose names from their own ethnic tradition. Thus, Biblical and Celtic names seem to be popular far beyond the boundaries of the appropriate ethnic groups. I must confess an especial interest in seeing how Celtic names, such as Kevin, Patrick,[3] Maureen, Eileen and Sheila, have become part of the common pool of given names—thus forcing those seeking an explicit Celtic heritage to fall back on names such as Moyra, Deirdre, Sean, Seamus and Liam.

Whether in the next two to three decades changes in such indicators will be measurable or measured remains to be seen, but at least they do provide sign posts for those who expect a new kind of ethnicity to appear on the American scene.

4. LANGUAGE MAY VERY WELL BE THE KEY ISSUE, for if those young people who want to evolve a self-conscious ethnic iden-

tity for themselves are willing to go through the hard work of learning a foreign language, then one must be willing to accept the fact that they are doing something more than posing. I am not sure, however, that the discomforts of and need to "personalize" a technocratic society are such that very many young people are going to try to learn Polish or Lithuanian or even Italian—much less, heaven save the mark, Gaelic.

One of the most intriguing aspects of the possible "new tribal" ethnicity is that it may disconcert the old "ethnic" traditions. Thus, at one university I know of, there is a Polish student union which is quite consciously concerned about Polish culture and which insists on holding its official meetings in Polish, much to the discomfiture and astonishment of the less ethnically self-conscious Poles in the university who find themselves alternately fascinated and repelled by such weird goings on. They are Polish, of course, but they see little point in wanting to speak the language that their poor old grandmother speaks and which, for their parents, represents an immigrant experience that they would like to forget.

The survival of ethnicity as a cultural social force in American society—which must be taken into account by any serious social analyst—does not depend on the "tribal" version of ethnicity. But if the new tribalism grows, then in years to come the ethnic factor will be even more important than it is today.

Notes

1. I do not subscribe to such an analysis of contemporary American life, nor do I believe in the existence of the "establishment" (though, if there were one, most of the young people who are really against it would be considered by the other members of American society to be part of it). I am more inclined to think that the revolt against technology has been affected by the availability of time and categories of thought which make the revolt possible. I am, needless to say, delighted that what one of my students called "empiriological imperialism" of science has been overturned. I am equally glad that, as another student put it, "science has been put back in its place" but, as someone who makes some claim to being an empiricist (a "naïve" empiricist according to one of my students), I am appalled that the baby is being thrown out with the bath.

2. I am told that many native Africans are somewhat puzzled by the dress and hair-do of American blacks (many of whom, by African standards, are white rather than black). It is a reaction not dissimilar to that of the Irishman who finds the cultural enthusiasm of some of the American Irish both naïve and embarrassing.

3. Not really Celtic.

Chapter 13.
The Alienation of White Ethnic Groups

The angle of vision from which white ethnic groups view their present posture toward society is distinctly their own. But before I attempt to describe this view, let me make some observations about white ethnic groups in general.

1. They are not far removed from their immigrant experience. A few years ago half the adult Catholics in the country were either immigrants or the children of immigrants; if we include the third generation, the overwhelming majority of the Catholic population still has one foot in the world of the immigrant ghetto. Where there are large concentrations of a given ethnic group, and in most cities there are such concentrations, the churches, the journal organizations, newspapers and political organizations maintain a high level of nationality consciousness. The ethnics, therefore, tend to be well aware of and indeed proud of the fact that they are "different" from the rest of American society. However, they are not sure that the whole society accepts them. It was not so long ago that serious doubt was expressed about whether they or their parents could really be full-fledged Americans. More recently, many of them felt the need to demonstrate that they were superpatriots—more "American" than anyone else, and within the last decade John F. Kennedy was almost denied the presidency largely because of his religion.[1] Ethnics, then, are caught between a powerful loyalty to the United States and deep insecurities about whether they are even now accepted by the Republic.

2. In addition to the social insecurity that comes from being still relatively close to the immigration experience, ethnics tend to be economically insecure. Presumably those under forty cannot really expect a return of the great depression, though the "invisible scar" of the great depression seems to be more vivid

among those social groups which suffered most from it. However, the basic economic insecurity of white ethnics is somewhat different. I would guess that it takes at least two generations of affluence before a group is able to take for granted that their affluence is not in jeopardy, and also before they are able to live with the disappointing reality that affluence brings its own frustrations.

At least some members of ethnic groups, in addition, feel that they are caught in an unfair economic bind with increased taxes and inflation eroding their real income. The state income taxes now being adopted all around the country generally tend to be regressive and to fall hardest on the lower, middle and working classes. Given the fact that much of the tax increase, at least at the state and local level, is earmarked for one form of welfare program or the other and that large (though perhaps not large enough) amounts of federal moneys are also going into such welfare programs, we can understand why ethnics feel that they are being taxed more heavily to subsidize other social groups. They will argue that no such subsidies were ever offered to them.[2]

3. They are profoundly committed to family, home and neighborhood in a fashion that those of us who are part of the cosmopolitan elite find very difficult to understand. Whether these commitments are a residue of present longing for blood and soil, or rather, constitute a symbol of being part of middle-class American life, is quite beside the point. A house, its landscaping and lawn, a barbecue pit in the back yard, the neighbors across the street, the playground where their children play, the church to which the family goes are parameters of life that are of immense importance in an ethnic community. In a well-to-do section on the South Side of Chicago that I served as a curate for a decade, young people, when they were asked where they were from, did not use the name of the neighborhood (Beverly Hills) or of the street (Ninety-fifth Street, Eighty-seventh Street, Seventy-ninth Street), but of the parish in which they lived. The community, be it noted, was a third generation, college-educated Irish neighborhood. Nevertheless, the investment of personality, selfhood and future life plans in the street in which one lived,

the church which one attended and the neighborhood of which one was a part was intense, and at times all important. A neighborhood is an extension of a man's home; and in a sense far beyond the trite use of the words—his home is his castle and his fortress. A threat to home and neighborhood is a threat to the very core of his personality.

The economic issue cuts across the neighborhood one, for in addition to having invested himself in his home and neighborhood, the white ethnic has also invested a good deal of his financial resources. Given the feeling of financial insecurity that is still very much with him, the home symbolizes his selfhood in two respects: it represents his personal and familial security and also his financial and economic security. A threat to the home and to the neighborhood is a threat of utter destruction.

It is extraordinarily difficult to persuade such a man that the arrival of other social groups in his neighborhood is not a threat. By any realistic standards he knows, it is a threat; for in other neighborhoods where these social groups have come the neighborhoods have ultimately been "destroyed"—that is to say, the prior inhabitants have been forced to move, frequently after suffering a substantial financial loss. We may tell him that it is the "block busters" who create panic that are responsible for the deserting of the neighborhoods. We may tell him that careful studies show that over the long run property values go up, not down, after black in-migration. We may even tell him that statistics show only a minor increase in crime at the first sign of black in-migration. He may or may not believe such statements, but for him they are irrelevant. His home, his family, his "piece of turf," his little physical corner of the universe is being threatened, and the elite groups who seem to control society are telling him that those who are threatening him have every right to do so, and indeed, ought to be encouraged to do so, but that he has no right, legal, social and moral, to defend himself and that which he values; that indeed, he is a white ethnic racist for even thinking that he should try to protect his corner of the universe from destruction.

The failure of the liberal elites to understand, much less to have compassion for this reaction, is the greatest single proof of their tendency to snobbishness with regard to the white ethnics. I do not pretend to know how the problem of changing neighborhoods can be resolved, but I am appalled at the thought that it is so casually dismissed as a manifestation of white ethnic racism.

4. Much of the rhetoric of social reform currently being used in the United States is not only lost on white ethnics, but actually creates a greater sense of alienation and confusion among them. We must remember that these groups are but a generation or two away from the Old World; to be told that they are responsible or ought to feel guilty over the plight of the Negroes puzzles them, when it does not make them angry. It was not their ancestors who brought the black slaves to this country; it was not their ancestors who kept them enslaved until a century ago; it was not their ancestors who arranged the disgraceful national compromise whereby slavery was replaced with serfdom; it was not their ancestors who enacted the Jim Crow laws; it was not their ancestors who imported the blacks to the big cities of the North as cheap labor. They may not like blacks—they may be afraid of them—but it seems to them that they are being asked to pay the heaviest price for social wrongs for which they have relatively little responsibility. Furthermore, they are close enough to the memory of their own immigrant poverty to realize that reform groups were not particularly concerned about them. Those social classes which seem so committed to expiating guilt for injustices done to the blacks were quite unconcerned about injustices and exploitations worked upon white ethnics and upon their ancestors. No one ever worried about the Polish poor or the Irish poor, and no one seems to worry very much now about the residual poverty groups in both these populations.

Let me emphasize once again that I am not committing myself to this particular line of argument, but I am saying that unless we understand a) that many white ethnics think this way with some justification, and b) that their feelings represent an important dimension of social reality, we shall never be able to come to grips with the problems of unity in our large cities.

5. White ethnics are afraid of violence. There was much of it in their own past, both in this country and in Europe. They

have worked hard to achieve a modicum of economic and social security. They now have much more to lose than they did in the past. The threat of violence implies that their efforts may have been in vain, and that their hard-won gains are in jeopardy. It is no doubt true that most of them have not been the victims of violence, and that their only contact with violence is what they see on the mass media. It is also true that subconsciously they may have guilt feelings about the exploitation of blacks, and that there may be "racial memories" out of the past which make them afraid of strangers. But having conceded these points, I must still insist that violence in American cities is real. Many streets are unsafe, most parks are unsafe—not only at night but all day; quiet residential neighborhoods are open to easy attack, and the threat of violent eruption hangs over the city each summer. Those of us who are more sophisticated may console ourselves with the thought that those threats—to burn the city down or to tear it up or to engage in guerrilla warfare—in which some black militants indulge are meant mostly for internal consumption among blacks, and do not represent the real intentions of the militant leadership. We could even argue that when there are riots, the militants are as surprised as anyone else. This may console us—it may even be true—but it is not likely that white ethnics will be all that sophisticated. When a member of the Black Panther party postures like Mussolini on the television screen and warns that he is going to destroy a city, the white ethnics are quite prepared to take him at his word.

There are many responses that we have offered to the law and order issue, all of them patently inadequate. We have said that our nation has had a violent past. We have argued that violence —physical as well as psychological—is done daily to the black population. We have said that the so-called crime waves are exaggerated and have pointed out the many weaknesses in the uniform crime statistics in the Federal Bureau of Investigation. All of these arguments are quite correct, but they will do nothing to lessen the fear of violence among white ethnics. Nor does the tendency of the liberal cosmopolitan elite to scapegoat the police make much of a contribution to lowering their fears. Let us concede that the police forces of our urban centers are in great need of professionalization and modernization. Let us concede that there are far too many psychopaths on the police force. Let us concede that the blacks have every reason to look upon many police as their bitter enemies. Nevertheless, to a population obsessed with the fear of violence, the police are the only barrier standing between them and violence. Just as the liberal elites frequently seem all too ready to demand that white ethnics turn their neighborhoods over to invaders (while the elite neighborhoods are quite safe), so it frequently seems, too, that the liberal elites, secure in their suburban bastions, are demanding that the white ethnics even be denied effective protection from violence by adequate police forces.

The failure of the elites to understand the relevance of the law and order issue has been a disastrous political and social mistake, not merely because it has been used by demagogues to win elections but because the liberal elites, by denying the problem, have turned its solution over to the demagogues and failed to make much in the way of an intelligent contribution towards a solution. There ought to be no reason why the streets and parks of our large cities are unsafe. If it will take massive funds and massive improvement of the quality of the police to bring safety and peace to the metropolis, then so be it. It ought to have been the function of liberal elites to stress these points rather than to leave the field to those who think that law and order can be established simply by "cracking down." [3]

6. The white ethnics are deeply committed to American society. While the society may not yet have completely accepted them, they are close enough in memory to the poverty and tyranny in their own pasts to be extremely grateful to a nation which has provided them with both affluence and political freedom. For example, they do not like the war in Vietnam any more than anyone else and yet because of their commitment to the United States, they are, I should think, less likely to be certain that the war is unjust than are other more established groups within the society. Furthermore, they are completely incapable of understanding student protesters. Time after time after time I have heard them say, "Those kids are so lucky to

get a college education. Why are they attacking the college that's educating them? If they don't like it, they can always get out." The white ethnic simply cannot understand the "quality of life" and "participation" arguments that the student protesters use, nor can they understand a word of the pseudo-Marxist jargon which is the typical rhetoric of the student left. From the white ethnic viewpoint, the students are much worse than the blacks because the blacks at least do have real problems about which to protest. But the students have no problems at all and are simply spoiled children of the rich who would benefit greatly from a sound thrashing. When the ethnics stop to think about it, they're also inclined to argue that these are the very children of those elite groups who are demanding that they, the ethnics, yield their neighborhoods to the blacks and pay higher taxes in order to fund black attacks on their neighborhoods and their cities. This makes them more angry at the students.

Even if the massive urban riots are now a thing of the past, the law and order issue will remain extremely important among white ethnic groups as long as government and universities are unable to prevent small groups of violent protesters from disrupting university life. When what the ethnics view as a handful of "spoiled brats" bring turmoil to great universities, the ethnics are driven into cold fury.

The notion of some of the student left that they can fashion an alliance with the ethnic working class simply reveals how little these young people understand the ethnics.

7. While there are few things more valued by ethnics than a college education, there are also few things which they suspect more than intellectualism. In this respect, of course, they are typical of the rest of American society which concedes high status to a college professor but is extremely suspicious of ideas and expends great amounts of money on its universities but doesn't trust what goes on in the universities. Just as the white ethnic is unlikely to be happy at the possibility that his taxes are subsidizing social groups bent on destroying his own neighborhood, so he does not take kindly to the idea that his taxes are being used to subsidize faculty radicals and student nihilists on the university campus. The moral and intellectual arrogance

of these faculty and students as displayed in the mass media merely confirms the ethnic in something he has always suspected—all the education professors receive doesn't guarantee that they have much common sense (a fact which many of us would not disagree with). At the same time, the ethnic is unhappily aware that the "professor" and the "expert" are increasingly powerful in American society.

8. The ethnic is also deeply concerned about primary and secondary education since all of his children will attend at least these schools. He is as conscious as anyone else that the quality of public education in the large cities is deteriorating despite the increased moneys that are being spent. He assumes, although with little justification, that this increase in costs and deterioration in quality is related to the presence of large numbers of blacks in the public school system, blacks who appear to him to be more interested in protesting and demonstrating or engaging in vandalism than they are in getting an education. So not only are the blacks bent upon destroying his neighborhood, they are also bent upon destroying the public school system. It is all well and good for the suburban liberal elites to talk about integrating the school systems for they can send their children to safe, high quality suburban schools or alternately to private schools. Once again the elites are bent on improving the lot of the blacks at no cost to themselves and at considerable cost to the white ethnics. Let us concede, of course, that there are many holes in this argument, and yet if we cannot understand why ethnics might think this way, we miss the whole point of the present crisis of unity in the cities.

I should say something also about the Catholic schools. Protestant and Jewish leaders have persisted in believing for a long time that Catholic schools were something forced on an unwilling Catholic population by their ecclesiastical leadership. If Catholics had their choice, it was argued, they would choose to send their children to public schools like other Americans. More recently, some Catholic educators not excluding bishops have tried to persuade themselves that the popularity of Catholic schools is declining among American Catholics. Unfortunately for both arguments the empirical data reveal exactly the opposite. Catholics were and are overwhelmingly sympathetic towards Catholic education. Furthermore, there is no evidence of substantial transfers from public schools to Catholic schools for racial reasons—despite the attempt of at least one civil liberties organization to propagate such a myth. Many of the white ethnics are deeply committed to Catholic education for their children no matter what the cost. They do not take kindly and never did to the failure of the state to provide some sort of support for Catholic schools. When the ethnics now observe that liberal elites are sympathetic to the subsidization of black education but still oppose the subsidization of Catholic education, they become quite angry. There are, of course, constitutional difficulties, but the ethnic might be forgiven for feeling that if the elites really wanted to help Catholic schools they could find constitutional ways of doing it.

9. The ethnic groups tend to be conservative both morally and religiously, as indeed is the overwhelming majority of American society, if one is to believe the data gathered by most survey research. The "permissiveness" or the "sexual revolution" or the "death of God" about which we read so much are, it would appear, limited to some divinity school faculties, the Broadway theater and sensational journalism. Nevertheless, permissiveness, the death of God and the sexual revolution are all associated in the minds of ethnics with the liberal cosmopolitan elites who may very well be allied with the black militants and the student protesters in an attempt to tear apart American society and to destroy the still very tentative security and affluence at which the white ethnics have arrived. There is, quite certainly, a touch of paranoia about all of this, but it is not only among white ethnic groups that paranoia seems to be rampant in contemporary America. If liberals have their Establishment to use as an inkblot and radicals their "military-industrial complex," if blacks and black sympathizers have their white racism on which to blame every problem, who are we to deny the ethnics their own private series of inkblots?

10. Finally, the ethnics find themselves increasingly isolated from their own political leadership. In cities like Chicago where patronage and a precinct organization still maintain some sort

of communication between the grass roots and the city hall, the problem is less acute than it is in cities where so-called "good government" has cut the liberal elites who run the city off from the ethnic hinterlands. But even in cities where ethnic politics is still a way of life, the alienation of white ethnics from their leadership is growing more intense. The political leadership, faced with grave social problems, is forced to fall back on experts and technicians for solutions; and it is precisely these experts who are most likely to arouse suspicions among the white ethnics and indeed to recommend programs that are most likely to confirm the ethnics' suspicions. Given the increased alienation of the ethnics from a governmental leadership which they feel is unaware of their problems or is exploiting them to solve the problems of others, the astonishing thing is that the so-called backlash vote is generally so small, at least in presidential elections. The conservatism of the ethnics probably makes them reluctant to run the risk of switching from their traditional political allegiance to vote for another party.

In summary, then, American ethnics in the large cities are afraid. They are afraid of what is going to happen to their homes, their families, their neighborhood, their economic and social security; they are afraid of violence; they are afraid of higher taxes; they are afraid of the dissolution of American society; they are afraid of black militants and student protesters; they are afraid of experts and professors; they are afraid of liberal do-gooders and planners; they are afraid of religious and moral corruption; they are afraid of being left out or ignored by those who have the real power in society; they are afraid that their schools and churches are being threatened; they are afraid that the most important values and realities of their lives are under heavy attack. Urban experts say they are wrong, but they don't think they're wrong, and at least until this point it must be confessed that the rest of us have done precious little to convince them that they're wrong. It will not help to lecture them about their prejudices nor to demand of their religious organizations that they engage in campaigns against prejudice. It will do no good to moralize, to pontificate, to lecture or to blame. We must first seek to understand, but whether we have the patience and the tact and the compassion to do so or not must be open to serious question. We must also, I think, realize that the desire to "participate," to have some control over one's own destiny is every bit as praiseworthy when it is manifested by one social group as when it is manifested by others. If demands for black power and student power are valid despite the distortions and the paranoia which sometimes accompany such demands, so, too, are the demands of ethnic groups for more power over the control of their own destiny, despite the bigoted and paranoid distortions with which such demands are sometimes presented.

Before we can do anything about any of this we must have more facts, and the facts are sadly lacking, even the facts that could substantiate as well as I would like, the assertions I have made in previous paragraphs. The first thing we must do is to learn more about the attitudes of white ethnics in our large cities and learn more about them from the "inside" and with some sense of sympathy and compassion. Research is not the magic answer to social problems, but research does, nevertheless, provide us with the raw material which is indispensable for fashioning social policy.

We must further recognize that ethnicity is a good thing, that ethnic differences provide richness and structure to a society, and that ethnic groups differ from our own (and surely we members of the liberal cosmopolitan elite do constitute a quasi-ethnic group). We must realize our own biases and snobbishness; we must understand that it is part of the human condition to be suspicious of people who are different from us. We must further realize that while we are busy trying to compensate for biases that run in one direction, we may overlook and even reinforce biases that run in other directions.

We must discover whether it is possible to establish some kind of communication with the best of the white ethnic leaders. We must recognize the tremendous importance of such problems as law and order, neighborhood security, taxes and the quality of education to elements of the population which feel they are increasingly cut off from their political leadership. We must ask whether it is necessary to meaningfully decentralize not only schools but many other dimensions of urban government. Daniel

Moynihan has suggested that the boroughs of London, made up as they are of several hundreds of thousands of people, might be extremely helpful models of meaningful urban decentralization.[4]

Finally, we might try to persuade some student leaders and some black militant leaders that they will not achieve their goals unless they are able to gain allies and some consensus among other groups in American society. In the final analysis, attempts to obtain social change through blackmail threats of violence will lead only to repression. Some of the militant leaders have made it perfectly clear that it is repression they want because they think that such repression will then move American society into a prerevolutionary phase. Again, I can only marvel at their naïveté and lack of education. But hopefully, at least some of the more moderate student and black leadership will understand that at some point compromise and consensus is the essence of the political process.

These are but hints about directions in which we might move to respond to the problems of white ethnics. We will not get answers to the problem unless we are willing to put in substantial amounts of time, thought and money.

I am not hopeful. Black militants will continue to posture before the television camera threatening the white ethnics with violence. Students will continue to parrot their obscure Maoist line. Demagogues will continue to exploit the fears of those who feel threatened and alienated. New financial approaches will not be found to ease the tax burden on the middle class.

Social and intellectual elites will continue to use the stereotype "white ethnic racists" and to disdain the fears, the anxieties and the worries of a substantial segment of the urban population. Under such circumstances, I continue to be astonished that the alienation is not greater than it is. I do not anticipate an ethnic fascism in this country nor much violence from white ethnic organizations. I do not anticipate a political revolt. People do not revolt, they do not become fascists, at least I do not think they do, for social-psychological reasons. Whatever their fears, and they are serious, the white ethnics are still well fed and well clothed and well housed. Their children still can get into schools, whatever the quality of the schools may be. The white ethnics will complain, they will shift more and more to right-wing voting patterns, but they are not likely, in my judgment, to tear apart the consensus, tattered as it may be, on which our society still rests. Such a prediction may bring us some consolation, but if it persuades us that we do not have serious problems with the white ethnic groups, then we are blind and leaders of the blind.

On the other hand, if political, economic or military disaster should afflict the country, then we must face the serious prospect of a militant, violent, quasi-fascist political movement among the white ethnic groups. Such disasters are unlikely, but they are not impossible. Whether we can afford to ignore the possibility is a question that those of us who are responsible for providing intellectual and social leadership in American society must honestly face. My grim conclusion is that we will not do so.

Notes

1. The University of Michigan researchers estimated that Kennedy lost 5,000,000 votes because of his religion.

2. Let me emphasize once again that I am not necessarily agreeing with these arguments. They may not be factually true, or if they are factually true, they may not be socially relevant from the point of view of eliminating poverty in the country. However, the fact that many white ethnics think that such arguments are true and relevant becomes in itself an important reality and must be dealt with.

3. The classic example of the strange attitude toward these problems manifested by many cosmopolitan Americans was expressed by a chaplain of a certain college. I had remarked to him that while I did not approve of police violence, I still understood that police work was extremely dangerous in certain areas of the city and could understand the fears and insecurities of the police. He replied that he had thought of this too, and at first it had troubled him. But then he realized that the policeman had chosen his own profession and so had freely entered into a world of violence, while the blacks had not chosen to be born in the neighborhoods where they were born and had no options in the matter. "So," he added, "I don't feel so bad anymore about violence done to the police." Such a line of reasoning apparently soothed his Quaker conscience. It did not, however, notably

decrease the danger of police work nor increase professional standards or skills by which police can cope with such dangers.

4. See Gilbert Chesterton's *Napoleon of Notting Hill,* a book which ought to be required reading for anyone who thinks seriously of urban decentralization.

Chapter 14.
The Future of Ethnic Groups

It is now time to address ourselves to three general questions: 1) Are ethnic groups likely to survive in American society? 2) Can anything be done to mitigate ethnic conflicts? and 3) What kind of research would help shed some of the light we need on this subject?

As to the first question—whether ethnic groups have a future in American society—the previous chapters have, I hope, provided sufficient answer. There is no reason to think they will not continue to play an important role, at least for the rest of this century, despite the fact that the compositions of the groups are changing, as well as the kind of identification they provide for their members. (Joshua Fishman, in his large and impressive study of language loyalty,[1] indicates that there is apparently an inevitable decline across generation lines in the use of a foreign tongue, although he and many of his coauthors entertain some hope that the decline can be arrested and even reversed.)

Although immigration has by no means come to an end, and hundreds of thousands of immigrants enter the United States each year, the ratio of immigrants to the total population is obviously much smaller than it was at the turn of the century. And while the new immigrants do provide clients for the hard core of purely ethnic services (especially the press and radio programs identified with the mother tongue), they no longer represent the major focus of concern for most American ethnics.

Poles, Norwegians and Italians, for example, are far more concerned with shaping their future within the American environment than preserving their cultural links with the past. The cultural links are preserved, however, in two fashions—first, by the unconscious transmission of role expectations, some rooted in the past and others in the early experience in this country; and second, through a scholarly or artistic interest in the customs of the past. Thus, though the ethnic groups in this country have taken on a life of their own, more or less independent of the national cultures and societies where their roots lie, many of the old links survive, indirectly and undeliberately, or in a highly self-conscious academic fashion.

Again we can see how blurred the picture is and how difficult it is to be confident in the absence of more careful research. The American Irish are different, let us say, from the American Poles in part because they come from different cultural backgrounds, in part because they came to the United States at different times, in part because the two groups have had vastly different experiences in the American society, and in part because there are conscious efforts—at first from an intense determination to survive, and later out of leisurely academic and artistic interests —to keep a lot of the traditions and customs of the past.

The American Irish, I suspect, are only slightly moved by the current Londonderry riots in which Catholics in the north of Ireland have adopted some of the tactics of American blacks in their own civil rights movement. Not long ago, during a visit to a Catholic girls' college in the heartland of America, I noticed a sign on the bulletin board announcing that the Irish Club of the college would shortly hold its monthly meeting. I asked the young lady who was showing me through the college if she belonged to the Irish Club; it turned out that she not only belonged, she was its president. "Peggy," I asked her, "do you know what the six counties are?" She admitted that she did not. "Have you ever heard of the Sinn Fein?" She had not. "Have you ever heard of the Easter rising, or the I.R.A.?" She conceded her ignorance. Finally, I said "Peggy, do you know who Eamon de Valera is?" She brightened. "Isn't he the Jewish man that is the Lord Mayor of Dublin?" she asked.

And yet Peggy is Irish, and proudly so, though she is part of the fourth generation. She might be hard put to say specifically how she differs from her Polish classmates, but the political style of her family, the shape of its commitment to Roman Catholicism, perhaps even its interpretation of the meaning of the good life, are rooted in the Irish past; and even though Peggy later married a boy with a German name (it was all right, her relatives assured me, because his mother was Irish), she continues to be Irish, and I suspect her children will too, no matter what their name happens to be.

For Jews, the issue of ethnic identity is, it seems to me, even more subtle and complex. The horrifying disaster of the Second World War made most Jews much more explicitly conscious of their background and cultural traditions, and the existence of Israel as a modern nation state embodying these traditions reinforces this consciousness. Thus, while Jews are one of the most thoroughly acculturated groups in American society, they are also extremely conscious of their origins and history, and even in the third and fourth generation they make greater efforts to preserve their own culture than any other major immigrant group.

Intermarriage and Identity

Those who doubt that ethnic groups have much of a future usually point to intermarriage as proof that ethnicity is vanishing on the American scene. The truth is, however, that there is almost nothing in the way of detailed literature on ethnic intermarriage except the studies on intermarriage between Jews and gentiles.[2]

Harold Abramson's study, referred to in Chapter 7, finds that ethnic intermarriage does, indeed, increase with generation, education and occupational success. But ethnic intermarriage hardly seems to be a random event. A typical ethnic in Abramson's population was some two and one-half times more likely to choose a mate from his own ethnic group than he would if ethnicity were irrelevant in a choice of spouse. Furthermore, even intermarriage seems to take place along certain ethnically predictable lines—that is to say, if someone does marry outside his ethnic group, he is more likely to choose someone from a group considered relatively close to his own. Thus an Irishman, for example, is much more likely to marry a German than a Pole or an Italian.

Abramson's data, which were collected for another purpose,

do not supply the answers to two critical questions. First, what sort of ethnic identification, if any, does the new family choose for itself? While there is not much in the way of precise data, impressionistic evidence (reported by Moynihan and Glazer) seems to indicate that a choice of ethnic identity is made either by the spouses themselves or by their children.

The second and more complicated question is: Which traits are passed on to which children in an ethnic intermarriage? Let us consider, for example, the apparent political liberalism of the Irish in comparison with the other Catholic groups described in the previous chapter. In a marriage between an Irish male college graduate and a Polish female college graduate, holding all the other variables constant, whose social attitudes are likely to affect the children? Will the father, rather than the mother, prevail because the father is political leader of the family? Will the father influence his sons and the mother her daughters, or will the flow of influence be vice versa? Or will it all cancel out, with the Polish-Irish children assuming positions on social issues somewhere between those of the two ethnic groups?

Of course we also have no way of knowing whether the social attitudes reported in the previous chapter will survive into the next generation, even in ethnically endogamous marriages. These complicated questions simply underscore how precious little we know about the later stages of acculturation and assimilation. What we do know, however, scarcely justifies the popular assumption that the ethnic groups are disappearing.

But if they are likely to persist, how is society to cope with the problems that ethnicity generates? For it seems to me we must, above all, recognize that ethnic problems are also likely to persist, and that it does little good to lament them or moralize about them. We must also be carefully aware of our own ethnic biases and not permit ourselves the luxury of superior attitudes towards behavior which, if the truth be told, we dislike mostly because it's not the sort of thing "our kind of people" might do. And thirdly, we must be wary of turning correlations into causes. In Chapter 6, for example, we described correlations between "Polishness" and certain ethnocentric attitudes. It would be quite easy to make a leap and say that being Polish "causes" the ethnocentric attitudes—and some Polish critics of the data I've discussed have assumed I was making such a leap, even though there were no grounds for such an assumption. There may be something in the Polish cultural background to explain anti-Semitism, but there is nothing I can think of that would explain racism. Thus, I would be much more inclined to see the conflict between the Poles and the blacks in terms of the particular stage in the ethnic assimilation process that the Poles happen to have reached at the time when the black group has become militant. In other words, I am inclined to think we can explain the conflict between the Poles and the blacks almost entirely in economic, social and psychological terms, without having to fall back on cultural traditions at all.

The problem is not much easier with respect to the somewhat less intense controversies separating white ethnic groups, one from another. I have no clear notions of how to cope with an apparent increase in Jewish animosity toward Catholics in recent years (see Tables 1–4 in Appendix) or with the antagonism between Irish Catholics and other Catholic groups. I suspect we need intergroup dialogue, cultural exchanges and serious interest in the cultural institutions of those groups with which we are most likely to compete. I am also inclined to think we need leaders who are less demagogic since ethnic groups seem to have a genius for flocking to demagogic leadership. And we must show great self-restraint in attacking the leadership of other groups, even though that leadership is likely to leave itself wide open to such attacks. But having repeated suggestions which must be considered as little more than truisms of intergroup work, I am at a loss as to how to proceed further. We simply do not know enough; not enough data are available, not enough experiments have been done, and all too few theories have been advanced to enable us either to understand what is going on or to prescribe remedies for the pathology we may observe.

It does seem to me, however, that it is essential for political leaders, social planners and influential figures in the ethnic communities to abandon the rather foolish controversy of whether ethnicity is a good thing or a bad thing—particularly since it clearly has both good and bad effects—and settle down to a better understanding of what it means and how we may live with it, not merely tolerably, but fruitfully.

A number of people have made some concrete suggestions for helping to "cool" the tensions among America's ethnic groups. Some try to deal with the problems "where they're at," that is, at the actual point of collision. The American Arbitration Association, for example, has organized a new Center for Dispute Settlement which will offer free mediation and arbitration services to help resolve differences between racial and ethnic groups, students and school administrators, landlords and tenants, businessmen and consumers, and other groups involved in clashes that might otherwise escalate into dangerous confrontations.

Others address themselves to efforts to get at the underlying causes. If competition for scarce, or presumably scarce, opportunities and services is at the root of much of the conflict among ethnic groups, they reason, one way to reduce such conflict is to "enlarge the pie" through economic and social programs aimed at improving the overall quality of life for all Americans. Such proposals have come from a variety of sources, including the carefully detailed Freedom Budget, outlined a few years ago by economists Leon Keyserling and Vivian Henderson and others, and the broad *Agenda for the Nation* published by the prestigious consultants of the Brookings Institution. All of these proposals envision a shift in national priorities to channel some of our enormous productive capacities into programs to provide jobs, schools, housing, recreation, health services and other essentials, not only for the hard-core poor who, in our less affluent past, have been consistently squeezed out in the competition for these needs, but also for the many millions of hard-working lower middle-class ethnics embittered by poor schooling, dead-end jobs and an unrelenting, unfair tax burden.

New Concepts, New Approaches

A few scholars and social activists are beginning to devise new strategies for working with ethnic groups. David Danzig of Columbia University, who was one of the first to write about group interests and their potential for intergroup conflict, points out that "only a generation ago, a good deal of the political life of the nation was fashioned in the image of just these [white ethnic] groups." Now, he explains, "ethnic groups are being relegated to a kind of expendable segment of the population." [3]

Danzig and others conclude that new social institutions are needed to replace those that are now obsolete. Once the labor union, the church and the political club served as intermediate structures between the individual and the complicated, anonymous society around him. There was someone people could tell their troubles to and know that something would be done for them. Today, both churches and unions have become large, bureaucratic organizations, and the political clubs have been replaced by "good government" reformers. In this age of punch cards and electronic switchboards it has become almost impossible to find someone to turn to for comfort.

How, then, can ethnic groups make their needs known? On the Northwest Side of Chicago and in South Philadelphia, both mixed white ethnic neighborhoods, and in an Italian neighborhood in the Bronx, there are new community organizations built around the problems of their members—not merely protectionist groups banding together out of fear and frustration, but people working for better housing, improved recreational facilities, consumer protection and similar needs common to all who live in the neighborhood.

Irving M. Levine, urban affairs director of the American Jewish Committee, suggests a number of such substantive issues around which ethnic Americans can rally. He points out, for instance, that it has been a mistake to allow the law-and-order issue to become a right-wing battle cry, and he thinks community groups should be encouraged to organize around "shaping a safer neighborhood" just as they have organized around schools, housing and welfare. In place of vigilantism, Levine has in mind developing among fearful groups a recognition of the new possibilities for fighting crime more effectively. Such things as "upgraded police training, sophisticated electronic devices and advanced communications . . . must become the focus of widespread public demand." [4]

Levine and others also urge some measure of tax relief as a response to the frustration that many ethnic Americans feel, and he urges labor, the churches and the community organizations to press for doubling the dependency allowance and for replacement of local school taxes by a graduated statewide tax. "Surely this is an issue that speaks for the needs of white ethnic America," he says, "and at the same time it may serve to equalize city and suburban school budgets, bringing benefits to black children as well as white taxpayers."

It is worth noting that Nat Hentoff, antiestablishment writer and social critic, also has picked up this theme: "Those on the Left," he writes, "ought to try to get inside the isolation of those whites making five to ten thousand a year and just hanging on. . . . 'The average white ethnic male' . . . needs tax relief, badly, and to get it, he might well join politically in a move to make taxation a good deal more equitable. . . . If he gets his, he won't be all that bugged about the blacks getting theirs, no matter what he thinks of them." [5]

The cost and quality of education is closely related to taxation, especially in the working-class suburban communities where many ethnic Americans now live. The schools in many of these communities are often woefully inadequate, as are the more deteriorated black schools in the inner cities. It is not altogether surprising that the residents of these communities object to the emphasis on upgrading black schools alone. As Levine points out, "the lower middle class . . . has been made to feel that it is they who must now sacrifice to remedy deficiencies in public education."

Jack Meltzer, of the University of Chicago Urban Studies Program, advocates "a 'Headstart' program to prepare advantaged children to welcome" disadvantaged children into their schools. In a somewhat different vein, Levine argues:

> While equality in education is still a fighting issue, and should occupy our time and conscience, in reality the widespread obsolescence of education is a more inclusive fight. The possibilities

opened up by effective decentralization and community participation, by computer technology, and by a widening of the choice
of educational options should be disseminated throughout ethnic
America and held up as models for new programs. The granting
of a per-pupil stipend might encourage new, competing educational systems, relieve the failure-oriented public school appara-
tus of the total burden and satisfy parents of parochial school
children (most of whom are ethnic whites) that their special financial problems are not totally disregarded.[6]

I am forced to comment, in passing, that when an American
Jewish Committee staff member can raise the possibility of alternatives to public education—alternatives which would be supported presumably by governmental grants—it is something of
an innovation. And, even though the American Jewish Committee remains steadfastly opposed to government aid to religious
schools, it should be clear to the reader that one most obvious
existing alternative to public education is parochial education
—which, incidentally, has an appeal of its own to many ethnic
Americans. If one combines these suggestions with Christopher
Jencks' call, in *The New York Times Magazine*,[7] for a subsi-
dized private education for black Americans, we have the begin-
nings of a program which, if it were seriously implemented,
would mean a drastic pluralization of American education.
There is much irony in these proposals, not the least of which is
that they hint at pluralization at the very time that many American Catholics are decrying their own separate school system.

The suggestions described above touch primarily on socioeconomic needs: personal safety, taxes, schools. But those searching
for answers to intergroup hostility are aware also of the deep
psychological needs for identity, community and belonging.
Robert Wood, former Undersecretary of the Department of
Housing and Urban Development and now head of the MIT-
Harvard Joint Center for Urban Studies, warns that economic
aid and a higher standard of living "bring no relief from loneli-
ness and anonymity. The cultivation of group, family, or kind,"
he says, "is a powerful support [against] the unbearable pressures of urban life." [8]

Levine, too, speaks to the issue of mental health in broader terms than psychiatry and organized treatment institutions. He describes "closed people who are moving in tunnels, frightened of a world where no one seems to be in control—least of all, themselves." And he calls on churches, unions and ethnic societies to undertake new forms of entertainment and leisure-time activities that counteract the inertia of the lower middle class, and to demand new public and private mental health programs, with the kinds of retreats and group settings that would help people open themselves up and deal with their anxieties.

I find myself deeply impressed with the courage and imagination that Levine and the others bring to this issue. The programs they propose will not, by themselves, solve the problem of conflict between blacks and white ethnics. They will not even be launched before many ideological prejudices among white liberals are overcome; but a beginning must be made somewhere, and certainly their suggestions represent the possibility, even the hope, of a beginning.

The American Jewish Committee has started a program of local and national consultations to bring together leaders of ethnic groups, educational institutions, religious structures, community-action agencies, mass media and civic and business organizations to study the implications of the rediscovery of ethnic America for the life of the nation. Out of such consultations, it is hoped, various programs would be developed to help ethnic leaders grapple with the problems of their own groups and of the larger society. Such action models, the Committee suggests, might include: an ethnic coalition committed to reducing intergroup tensions; a labor-supported community-action program for white workers; ethnic and cultural identity programs in mainstream institutions; new forms of fraternal, service and religiously sponsored activities; and projects to promote mass-media consciousness of ethnic America. Each program would be designed to address the problems of ethnic America, and its success would be measured by the degree to which group needs were met and group conflict decreased.

This program grows out of a tradition of coping with group problems in urban situations; it is a sophisticated tradition and one that has had considerable success in the past. Given enough money and enough patience, such approaches could make a major contribution to easing tensions both between black and white and among white groups. However, there is a new variable which must be taken into account, and which may force a drastic rethinking of the traditional model of intergroup work.

The white ethnic groups are no longer immigrant groups. They are no longer poor, depressed, downtrodden and uneducated. But despite a moderate financial and educational achievement, they are still deeply suspicious of "outsiders," particularly when these outsiders are "professors" or "intellectuals" or "experts." Presumably the parents and grandparents of these ethnics were also suspicious of outsiders, but lacking economic and educational resources, they were in no position to indulge their suspicions nearly as much as the present generation. The very fact that the ethnics have become acculturated, though not assimilated, will make them more, rather than less, difficult to work with.

It seems to me that it is up to the organized agencies within the ethnic groups to take the lead in cooperation. (I would even propose, for example, that Jewish agencies declare a moratorium on further research on anti-Semitic attitudes and instead find agencies of other ethnic or religioethnic groups with which they can cooperate in studying the much larger issue of interethnic animosity. In fact, as a general principle, I think no ethnic agency in the United States ought, at the present time, engage in research by itself, or solely on its own population.)

The Research Gap

I come back now to my own favorite theme—the urgent need for additional research in the entire area of ethnic relations. What sort of research is needed? There isn't *any* demographic socioeconomic or sociopsychological information about the latter stages of the acculturation process of American ethnic groups; it simply does not exist, and it is not likely to exist in the foreseeable future. There's a great likelihood that no attempt will be made to collect such information until it is too late. The Census Bureau now provides data only on the foreign born, and tells us nothing about the second, third or fourth-generation Americans. If one looks under "Ethnicity" in the indices of the behavioral science journals, one can find articles about Eskimos and Navaho, about tribes in Africa and New Guinea, even occasionally about black-white relationships, but precious little else. Ethnic questions are not routinely included in survey questionnaires, and for all the wild assertions about ethnic voting patterns (based usually on the foreign-born percentages of the Census tract data), national samples of political behavior rarely break down the American religious groups into their various ethnic components.

One is truly hard put to know why the last serious sociological study of American Poles was done by Thomas and Znaniecki in 1918. It could be, as one middle-aged Ph.D. from Columbia University suggested to me, that those who trained the present generation of younger American sociologists repressed the possibility of ethnic research from their consciousness because of their own profound ambivalence about their ethnic backgrounds.

In my judgment, we must collect a great deal of basic demographic and socioeconomic information which simply does not exist now. We must know who and where and what the major ethnic groups are—not merely the large groups we have spoken of here, but also the smaller groups, which may be even more instructive for understanding a multiple-melting-pot model of society—the Greeks, the Armenians, the Luxembourgers, the Lebanese and others who are still very much with us and from whom there is a lot to be learned. Once we had the basic demographic information, we could go on to attitude and value studies, and the more complicated questions about the impact of ethnicity on social structure. (I say we could because, in all honesty, I don't really believe that we will. In fact, I don't even believe we are going to start putting ethnicity on survey research questionnaires as a standard item.)

Besides collecting basic demographic, socioeconomic and sociopsychological data about the American ethnic groups, I think we must do two other kinds of research: We must support graduate students who are willing to go into the ethnic ghettos that survive in our big cities, and even in our suburbs, and study closely the life styles and the role expectations of those who live in these ethnic communities. (Hopefully, the students will be operating out of the same general theoretical perspective, asking similar questions and periodically comparing notes with each other; unless this is done, we are not going to have the kind of raw material out of which survey questions can be formed to give us precise statistics about the different role expectations of ethnic groups.)

We also need to do case studies of both conflict and cooperation situations, so that we have some idea of what environmental and personal factors can turn competition into cooperation, or at least prevent it from becoming open conflict. I am inclined to suspect that since ethnic animosity is deeply rooted in the personality, psychiatry can make a major contribution to this sort of research.

Let me cite, for example, some very provocative data on Catholic-Jewish relations published in 1968 in a book by Martin Marty, Stuart Rosenberg and myself.[9] The data (see Tables 1–4 in Appendix) are based on two surveys conducted for the *Catholic Digest*—one by the Ben Gaffin firm in 1952, the other by the Gallup organization in 1965.

The most striking finding of the research is that in the thirteen years covered, there has been a downward shift in unfavorable feelings among Catholics towards Jews in all but two of the measures used, while among Jews unfavorable attitudes towards Catholics have increased in all but three of the measures. (In only one respect had attitudes on both sides improved at the same rate: willingness to vote for a member of the other group as President.)

In 1965, Jews were far more likely than they were in 1952, for example, to say they thought their own group was prejudiced against Catholics and that Catholics were prejudiced against Jews. They were also far more likely to express the feeling that Catholics do not respect Jewish beliefs, that Catholics do not want to intermarry, that Catholic clergy are not intelligent and do not promote understanding, that Catholic magazines are not fair. On five of these seven subjects, the Catholics' attitude towards Jews had become more favorable. Altogether the responses suggest that the two groups have switched places: In 1952, Catholics had a more negative attitude towards Jews than Jews did towards Catholics; by 1965 the reverse seemed to be true.

What is even more troubling is that this apparent increase in anti-Catholic feeling appeared to be concentrated among the younger and the more religious Jews. Moreover, the negative feelings occurred most often among the college-educated; they evidently did not stem from ignorance or lack of sophistication, and could not be counted on to go away in time.

Let me stress that we must be very cautious in interpreting this apparent change in Jewish attitudes towards Catholics. The Jewish sample of the 1952 survey was quite small, and though the size of the 1965 survey was large enough to permit some confidence in the accuracy of the data, the findings are nonetheless highly tentative and must be viewed with considerable reservation.

If, however, our sample is representative of the Jewish population, and *if* it continues to be representative when the Jews are divided into educational and age subgroups, then not only is there an increase in anti-Catholic feeling among American Jews, but this increase is most marked among college graduates and younger Jews and therefore seems likely to grow worse instead of better.

Indeed, if these phenomena are valid representations of reality, a very notable problem in Catholic-Jewish relationships may be facing us in years to come—particularly when Catholics, whose attitudes towards Jews appear to have improved substantially in the last ten years, discover that the reverse has happened among Jews. Such a discovery might lead to a resurgence of anti-Jewish feeling among Catholics; and the widespread optimism that an era of religious good will in the United States is about to begin may prove unjustified.

Some sociologists have claimed—I think without proper qualification—that among gentiles, particularly Protestants, religiousness is related to anti-Jewish feeling. I am not prepared, on the basis of the data cited above, to say that among Jews religiousness is related to increased anti-Catholic feeling—if indeed there be such an increase. But surely a minimal conclusion from these findings is that considerably more research is necessary on the subject of Catholic-Jewish relationships. Perhaps it also would not be inappropriate to suggest that Catholic and Jewish agencies join together to study the relationships between their two groups, and that it would be a mistake, in view of the findings just cited, to concentrate merely on anti-Jewish feeling among Catholics.

I want to emphasize again that it seems to me all these research efforts ought to be jointly sponsored by a number of ethnic agencies, whether by themselves or in cooperation with foundations and the Federal government. Indeed, research on the research project—that is to say, studies of how ethnic agencies cooperate in research projects—would itself make interesting investigation.

Notes

1. Joshua Fishman *et al.*, *Language Loyalty in the United States* (London and The Hague: Mouton, 1966).

2. Marshall Sklare, "Intermarriage and the Jewish Future," *Commentary*, April 1964, and Erich Rosenthal, "Studies of Jewish Intermarriage in the United States," *American Jewish Year Book*, Vol. 64 (1963), two of the best research reports on this subject.

3. David Danzig, "The Social Framework of Ethnic Conflict in America." Paper delivered at National Consultation on Ethnic America, Fordham University, June 20, 1968. (The American Jewish Committee.)

4. Irving M. Levine, "A Strategy for White Ethnic America." Paper delivered at Conference on the Problems of White Ethnic America, University of Pennsylvania, June 25, 1968. (The American Jewish Committee.)

5. Nat Hentoff, "Counterpolitics: The Decade Ahead," *Evergreen Review*, February 1969, p. 25.

6. *The Reacting Americans: An Interim Look at the White Ethnic Lower Middle Class* (New York: The American Jewish Committee, 1968), p. 27.

7. Christopher Jencks, "Private Schools for Black Children," *The New York Times Magazine*, November 3, 1968, p. 30.

8. *The Reacting Americans, op. cit.*, pp. 7, 14.

9. Martin Marty, Stuart Rosenberg and Andrew M. Greeley, *What Do We Believe?* (New York: Meredith Press, 1968).

Chapter 15.
Conclusion: Problem or Promise

As someone who has insisted for a decade and more that American social science ought to be concerned about the continuation of ethnicity in American society I have mixed feelings about the current fascination with the subject in academic, governmental, foundation and mass media offices. Obviously, I am delighted that people don't look at me as though I were crazy when I say that ethnic groups have survived in American society, but I am considerably less than pleased to discover that from a state of nonexistence white ethnic groups have become a social problem without anybody bothering to do any careful study in between. My feeling is that most members of American ethnic groups are going to be unpleasantly surprised to discover that they are a problem or that they are a "blue-collar problem" and, much worse, a "hard hat problem." As much of a shock as it may be to elite groups in American society, there are considerable numbers of white ethnics who are not blue-collar workers, and even substantial numbers who are college graduates and professionals; but they still have some recollection of what it was like to be a social problem, to be an object of the ministrations of welfare workers and settlement house do-gooders and they are, unless I am mistaken, quite disinclined to become that once again. Nor are they to be bought off by an increase in real income or by "community services." Indeed, the American white ethnics realize almost as much as do their black brothers that when the elite groups define you as a problem you are in for trouble. There was a time when the white ethnics had no choice but to be a "problem," but they have a choice now and I think they want no part of it.

Nonetheless, the elites persist in talking about the "blue-collar ethnic problem" and find themselves now joined by some of those alienated ethnics who only recently were seeking their own self-validation by crusading for rights for blacks. When the blacks made clear to them that they no longer could play their paternalistic roles, some of these leaders—most notably Catholic clergymen—rediscovered their own ethnic heritage and, with barely a change in vocabulary, they are now crusading for white ethnic rights. Indeed, one of them went so far recently as to observe that in a couple of years white ethnics would catch up to the blacks in matters of ethnic self-consciousness—a statement well calculated to offend, if possible, everyone.

In the final analysis, I suspect more harm will be done by this "social problem" approach than was done by simply ignoring the existence of white ethnic groups. It should be obvious by now that the perspective of this book assumes that ethnic diversity is an opportunity rather than a problem. Why the social problem approach is being emphasized and the "positive contribution" approach largely ignored is in itself a subject for further investigation.

The great theme of classical sociology is that in the last centuries Western society has moved from *gemeinschaft* to *gessellschaft*, from community to association, from primary group to secondary group, from mechanical solidarity to organic solidarity, from traditional authority to bureaucratic authority, from primordial drives to contractual drives. Weber, Durkheim, Tonnies, Toreltsch and Talcott Parsons have merely arranged different orchestrations on this architectonic theme. Under the impact of rationalization, bureaucratization, industrialization and urbanization, it is argued, the old ties of blood, faith, land and consciousness of kind have yielded to the rational structural demands of the technological society. In the conceptual framework of Professor Parsons's famous pattern variables, the immense social changes of the last two centuries have moved the race or at least the North Atlantic component of it from the particularistic to the universal, from ascription to achievement, from the diffuse to the specific. And other observers see a shift from the mythological to the religionless, from the sacred to the profane to the secular, from the folk to the urban. In other words, in organized society at the present time, the rational demands of the organization itself—or the organizations themselves—provide the structure that holds society together. Nonrational and primordial elements, if they survive at all, survive in the "private sphere" or in the "interstices." The old primordial forces may still be somewhat relevant in choosing a wife or a poker or bridge partner, but they have no meaning in the large corporate structures—business, labor, government, education, or even, for that matter, church. In the private sphere and in the interstices, the nonrational and primordial ties are seen as everywhere in retreat. Ethnic groups are vanishing, religion is losing its hold, men and women are becoming so mobile that they need no geographic roots. Professor Bennis [1] argues that there is emerging a "temporary society" made up of those members of the social elite for whom geographic, institutional and interpersonal stability are no longer necessary. These men, according to Bennis, move from place to place, occupation to occupation, and relationship to relationship without feeling any sense of personal or physical dislocation. Wherever they go, they are immediately able to relate intensely to their fellows, and when the time comes to terminate a set of relationships, they then enter into a new set that is equally intense but equally transitory. There is some suggestion in *The Temporary Society* that these new elites might even be capable of temporary marriage relationships. Whatever is to be said about the merits, moral, biological or aesthetic, of the temporary society, it is certainly the ultimate in the pilgrimage from *gemeinschaft* to *gessellschaft*. The lives of the denizens of the temporary society are completely shaped by the functional necessities of technological industrialism.[2]

In this official model of classical sociology, then, the primordial is seen to be on the way out. There may be some disagreement as to the speed of the evolutionary process, but nonetheless, secular man, technological man, religionless man, temporary man is seen as the man of the future. He is the one who occupies the critical positions in the government, in the media, in the university faculties, in the large corporate businesses. He needs little in the way of roots, nothing in the way of transcendental faith, and, as far as the technostructure is concerned, precious little in the way of emotion. Professor John

Schaar ironically describes the cognitive ideology of such a man. "Reality is that which is tangible, external, measurable, capable of being precisely conveyed to others; everything that is left over—and some might think that it is half of life—becomes curiously unreal or epiphenomenal. If it persists in its intrusions on the 'real' world, then it must be treated as trouble and those whose acts or motives are imbedded in the unreal world are treated as deviant cases in need of repair or reproof." [3]

Even if one does not wish to go quite that far in describing the pilgrimage from community to association, one still must admit that the implicit basic premises of most contemporary social analysis assume that the "public sphere" is the real world, that what goes on in corporate structures is what holds society together. The primordial or the tribal is limited to certain reactionary segments within the society and, even there, will be eradicated by the college educated in a generation or two.

The old right and the new left may disagree, but I think that an implicit value premise runs through much of this analysis: the rationalized society is not only the way things are but the way things should be. The primordial or prerational ties are seen as "unenlightened" and "reactionary." One need not discuss the current resurgence of interest in white ethnic groups very long without realizing that among many liberal academics there is a strong moral revulsion against ethnic groups. The term "white ethnic racist" is used much the same way as "damn Yankee" is used in the South. It becomes one word and indeed an epithet. An official of a national social work organization inviting me to give a speech at a meeting on the subject noted that "as far as I'm concerned, these people [white ethnics] are simply a barrier to social progress, though I suppose they have their own problems, too." And at the same conference a panel discussion about white ethnics labels them as "social conservatives." Serious discussions are held under the sponsorship of government agencies or private foundations in which the white ethnic "problem" is discussed as something about which "something must be done." One cannot speak to an academic group on the subject of ethnicity without some timid soul rising in the question period to inquire whether it might not be immoral to discuss the question of ethnic groups since ethnicity stresses the things which separate men and we ought to be concerned about those things which unite them. The bias in these reactions is apparent: the survival of the primordial is a social problem. The evolution from the nonrational to the rational, the sacred to the profane, the primordial to the contractual, the folk to the urban is seen not merely as a useful analytic model, but as profoundly righteous moral imperative. As some people have not completed their pilgrimage through this simple evolutionary model, obviously they are a social problem and "something must be done about them," such as, for example, seeing that their real income goes up at the rate of 5 per cent a year or providing day care centers for their neighborhoods. If one does enough of such things for them, maybe then they or at least their children will someday become more enlightened and be just like us.

It is certainly not my intention to deny the great utility of the official model of classical sociology. Obviously, a great transformation has come over the North Atlantic world since 1750. I need only to visit Ballendrehid, County Mayo, Ireland, to know that it is different from Chicago, Cook County, Illinois. The insight of the great sociologists is extraordinarily valuable but the trouble with their model as a tool for analysis is that the temptation is strong either to ignore or to treat as residual phenomena whatever can't be made to fit the model. I would contend that it is the very elegance of the official model of classical sociology that has blinded us to an incredibly vast range of social phenomena which must be understood if we are to cope with the problems of contemporary America.

I would suggest, then, that another model must be used either in conjunction with the official one or as the component of a more elaborate model which will integrate the two. According to this model, the basic ties of friendship, primary relationship, land, faith, common origin and consciousness of kind persist much as they did in the Ice Age. They are the very stuff out of which society is made and in their absence the corporate structures would collapse. These primordial, prerational bonds which hold men and women together have of course been transmuted by the changing context. The ethnic group, for example, did not even exist before the last of the nineteenth century. It came into existence precisely so that the primordial ties of the peasant commune could somehow or other be salvaged from the immigration experience. But because the primordial ties have been transmuted does not mean that they have been eliminated. They simply operate in a different context and perhaps in a different way. They are, according to this second model, every bit as decisive for human relationships as they were in the past. In fact, a strong case could be made that one primordial relationship— that of marriage—has in one respect become far stronger than it ever was in the past, because prospective marriage partners now require more rather than fewer ties of interpersonal affection; and while such ties of affection may appear structurally tenuous, they can be far more demanding on the total personality than were the structural ties of the past.

To the extent that this model has validity, a simple, unidimensional and unidirectional evolution from *gemeinschaft* to *gesellschaft* has not taken place. What has happened, rather, has been a tremendous increase in the complexity of society, with vast pyramids of corporate structures being erected on a substratum of primordial relationships. Since the primordial ties tend to be the infrastructure, or at least to look like the infrastructure to those who are interested primarily in corporate bureaucracies, it is possible to ignore them or at least to give them minimal importance. One does not, after all, think about the foundation of the Empire State Building when one sees it soaring into the air above Manhattan Island—not at least unless one happens to be an engineer.

From this second model, if it has any validity, one would conclude that the persistence of primordial bonds is not merely a social problem, but also a social asset. Communities based on consciousness of kind or common faith or common geography would be seen in this model not merely as residues of the past, but rather as a basic subcomponent of the social structure. Membership in such communities would be seen as providing personal identity and social location for members as well as making available a pool of preferred role opposites whose availability would ease stress situations at critical junctures in modern living. In other words, collectivities grouped around such primordial bonds would be seen not merely as offering desirable cultural richness and variety, but also as basic pillars of support for the urban social structure. A city government would view itself as fortunate in having large and diverse ethnic groups within its boundaries because such collectivities would prevent the cities from becoming a habitat for a "lonely crowd" or a "mass society." Psychologists and psychiatrists would be delighted with the possibilities of ethnic group membership providing social support and self-definition as an antidote to the "anomie" of the mass society. Another way of putting the same matter would be to say that to the extent the second model is a valid one, the lonely crowd and the mass society do not really exist.

But to what extent does the second model have any validity? My inclination would be to say that, if anything, much more research data can be fitted into the second model than into the first one. This is not the appropriate place to review in detail all the available evidence about the survival of the primordial, but one can at least list the principal research efforts. The now classic Hawthorne experiments of Elton Mayo and his colleagues demonstrated how decisive in the supposedly rationalized and formalized factory was the influence of informal friendship groups. Ruby Jo Reeves Kennedy proved in the early 1940's that there had been no change in patterns of religious intermarriage for a half century and thirty years later the research done at the National Opinion Research Center on young college graduates indicates that denominational (which includes Baptists, Lutherans, Methodists, etc., as separate denominations) intermarriage is still not increasing in the United States. The *American Soldier*,[4] showed how decisive personal loyalty was in holding together the combat squad. The work of Morris Janowitz and Edward Shils proved that the Wehrmacht began to fall apart only when the rank and file soldier began to lose faith in the paternalistic noncom who held his unit together. The voting studies of Paul Lazarsfeld and his colleagues proved that voting decisions were not made by isolated individuals but rather by members of intimate primary groups; and the similar studies of Elihu

Katz and others on marketing decisions and the use of innovative drugs showed how such decisions were strongly influenced by informal personal relationships. Will Herberg's classic, *Protestant, Catholic, Jew*, suggested a model explaining that religion is so important in the United States precisely because it provides self-definition and social location. James Q. Wilson's study of police discovered that sergeants of different ethnic groups have different administrative styles and the work of Edward Levine and others on the Irish as politicians has made clear—to those who are yet unaware of it—that the Irish have a highly instinctive political style (a political style, be it noted, that assumes the persistence and importance of primordial groups).

Manpower research done at NORC indicates that ethnicity is a moderately strong predictor of career choice. (Germans go into science and engineering, Jews into medicine and law, Irish into law, political science and history and the foreign service.) Studies of hospital behavior show that different ethnic groups respond differently to pain in hospital situations. (The Irish deny it and the Italians exaggerate it.) The Banfield and Wilson school of political science [5] emphasizes urban politics as an art of power brokerage among various ethnic and religio-ethnic groups. More recent research at NORC has shown that there is moderately strong correlation between ethnicity and a number of behavioral and attitudinal measures—*even when social classes have held constant*. Other research studies suggest that in large cities professional practice—medical, dental, real estate, construction—tend to be organized along religious or ethnic lines, and yet other work would indicate that some groups choose to create a form of self-segregation, even in the suburbs. Louis Wirth was right; there would indeed be a return to the ghetto but the ghetto would not be in Douglas Park (Chicago), it would be in Skokie and Highland Park (the suburbs).

I could go on, but it hardly seems necessary. Weep not for *gemeinschaft;* it is still very much with us. On the contrary, the burden of evidence ought to be on those who claim to see it vanishing. When it is argued that at least among the social elites secular, technological, religionless man seems to dominate, we need only point out that precisely the offspring of these elites seem presently most interested in recreating the tribal in the world of the psychedelic, neo-sacral communes. The model of classical sociology obviously is not to be abandoned, but it must be freed from a simple-minded, evolutionary interpretation. Furthermore, it is even more necessary to divest the model from the moralistic overtones which it has acquired in popular sociology and, unless I am very much mistaken, in professional sociology as well. To assume that religious or ethnic or geographic ties are unenlightened, reactionary, benighted or obscurantist is to make a moral judgment for which there are no grounds in serious social analysis.

The issue of the two models is not by any means just a theoretical one for, if one uses only the first model, then the angry white ethnic groups are seen basically as a social problem. But if one uses also the second model, one might conclude that ethnic loyalty could be a strong, positive force which might make available vitality and vigor for the preservation and enrichment of urban life for all members of the city. Thus, I would hypothesize that taking the propensity to desert the city as a dependent variable, one would find a strongly ethnic neighborhood scoring much lower on that variable than a cosmopolitan neighborhood. I would even go further and suggest that in an ethnic neighborhood under "threat" there would be less inclination to desert the city than in a less threatened cosmopolitan neighborhood. In one study of the 1969 mayoral election in Gary, Indiana, it was discovered that Poles who are more strongly integrated into the Polish community were more likely to vote for Mayor Hatcher than Poles who were less integrated into the ethnic community (though, obviously, in absolute numbers not many were likely to vote for him). There has been so little positive research done on the subject of white ethnic groups that one hesitates to state conclusively that ethnic identification and loyalty might be a positive asset for promoting social change in the city. Unfortunately, the rigid theoretical limitations of the official model have made it difficult to persuade funding agencies that such research might be appropriate. We are now faced with the rather bizarre situation in which many funding agencies are almost pathetically eager to do something about "the white ethnic problem," without ever having established that it is in fact a problem. It might be a distinct advantage.

If the second model has any utility at all, one could also call into question much of the romantic criticism and equally romantic utopianism of contemporary American society. It may turn out that there is, after all, rather little anomie. It may be that the mass society does not exist beyond Los Angeles and the university campuses around the country. It may be that the young who are seeking to create new clans, new tribes or new communes could achieve the same goals by moving back into their grandparents' neighborhood—an experiment which would also have the happy advantage of revealing to them that intimate communities can be narrow, rigid, doctrinaire and, in many instances, quite intolerant of privacy, creativity and diversity. If such romantic utopians would at least spend some time in their grandparents' neighborhood, they would be a bit more realistic about the problems that they will encounter in the Big Sur or along the banks of the Colorado River.[6]

American social scientists have to put aside their underlying assumptions if they are intelligently to investigate and understand ethnic pluralism in the large cities of our Republic. Social policy makers must likewise put aside most of *their* underlying assumptions. A considerable number of both the social scientists and social policy makers are currently announcing that black is beautiful (whether they really believe it or not is another matter) but if black is beautiful (and it is) then so is Irish, Polish, Italian, Slovenian, Greek, Armenian, Lebanese and Luxembourger.[7] All these represent valid and valuable cultural heritages. They all represent sources of identification and meaning in a vast and diverse society. They all have a positive contribution to a richer and more exciting human community.

Let me conclude with a story whose point I think I need not elaborate. I was standing in front of a church in the west of Ireland, camera in hand, attempting to record the church which I thought just possibly was the place of my grandfather's baptism. The parish priest, who was out cutting his hedge despite the rain, approached me, noted that I was a new man around here, and introduced himself. I must say I was a bit surprised when, on hearing my name, he remarked, "Ah, yes, you'd be the sociologist fellow from Chicago." Then he added, "Would you be wantin' your grandfather's baptismal record now?"

I admitted that the idea hadn't occurred to me. He shook his head in discouragement. "Ah," he said, "fine sociologist you are."

"Do a lot of people come seeking such records?" I asked.

He nodded gravely. "Indeed they do," he said, "indeed they do. Those poor people, you know, they've been in the States now for three generations and they come seeking roots; they want to know who they are; they want to know all about their past and their ancestors. The poor people, I feel so sorry for them. That's why I had all their baptismal records put on microfilm. It makes it a lot easier for people to find their roots."

Notes

1. Warren G. Bennis and Philip E. Slater, *The Temporary Society* (New York: Harper & Row, 1968).

2. To make my own biases in the matter perfectly clear, if I had to choose between the temporary society and a commune, I wouldn't have much difficulty choosing the latter.

3. John Schaar, "Reflections on Authority," *New American Review*, vol. 8, 1970, p. 671.

4. Samuel A. Stouffer et al., *The American Soldier: Adjustment During Army Life* (Princeton, N.J.: Princeton University Press, 1949).

5. See E. C. Banfield and J. Q. Wilson, *City Politics* (Cambridge: Harvard University Press, 1963).

6. I here rely heavily on a paper of mine, "The Positive Contributions of Ethnic Groups in American Society," which was done for the American Jewish Committee, 1968.

7. In Chicago we have a colony of Luxembourgers.

Appendix

Tables 1–4 are based on data collected in 1952 for the *Catholic Digest* by Ben Gaffin Associates and in 1965 by the Gallup organization for the same client. They were originally reported in Martin Marty, Andrew Greeley and Stuart Rosenberg, *What We Believe* (New York: Meredith Press, 1968).

Tables 5–8 are constructed for this volume from data collected in NORC's study of the effects of Catholic education. See Andrew M. Greeley and Peter H. Rossi, *The Education of Catholic Americans* (Chicago: Aldine Press, 1966).

Tables 9–14 are constructed for this volume from data collected in NORC's longitudinal study of June 1961 college graduates. See Joe L. Spaeth and Andrew M. Greeley, *Recent College Graduates* (New York: McGraw-Hill, 1970).

Tables 15–22 are constructed for this volume from NORC's study of integrated neighborhoods. See Norman Bradburn, Seymour Sudman and Galen Gockel, *Racial Integration in American Neighborhoods* (Chicago: Quadrangle Books, In Press).

I wish to express my gratitude to Professors Rossi, Spaeth, Sudman, Bradburn and Gockel for their cooperation in the construction of these tables.

TABLE 1
PERCENT OF DESIGNATED RESPONSES TO LISTED QUESTIONS ASKED OF RESPONDENTS AND CHANGE SINCE 1952

		Protestant	Catholic	Jewish	Protestant	Catholic	Jewish

Respect Beliefs of Others

A. "Do you think there is much ill feeling toward_____ among most people of your religious preference or not?"

	Percent Yes			Change Since 1952		
	Protestant	Catholic	Jewish	Protestant	Catholic	Jewish
Protestants	—	6	2	—	− 5	− 3
Catholics	19	—	30	− 5	—	+ 15
Jews	30	14	—	− 14	− 7	—

Look Down on

B. "Do you think_____look down on people of your belief?"

	Percent Yes			Change Since 1952		
	Protestant	Catholic	Jewish	Protestant	Catholic	Jewish
Protestants	—	17	16	—	− 5	0
Catholics	32	—	44	− 2	—	+ 14
Jews	14	14	—	− 6	− 4	—

Interfere

C. "Do you think that_____as a group try to interfere in any way with your religious beliefs or personal theories?"

	Percent Yes			Change Since 1952		
	Protestant	Catholic	Jewish	Protestant	Catholic	Jewish
Protestants	—	6	9	—	− 6	+ 5
Catholics	13	—	19	− 2	—	+ 6
Jews	2	3	—	− 2	− 1	—

Being Fair in Business

D. "Compared with most people of your religious beliefs, would you say that most_____are about the same, better, or not as good in being fair in business?"

	Percent Not as Good			Change Since 1952		
	Protestant	Catholic	Jewish	Protestant	Catholic	Jewish
Protestants	—	3	0	—	0	—
Catholics	5	—	1	− 1	—	− 2
Jews	28	23	—	− 11	− 8	—

Are Honest in Public Office

E. "Compared with most people of your religious beliefs, would you say that most_____are about the same, better, or not as good in being honest in public office?"

	Percent Not as Good			Change Since 1952		
	Protestant	Catholic	Jewish	Protestant	Catholic	Jewish
Protestants	—	4	0	—	− 2	− 1
Catholics	6	—	11	− 2	—	+ 8
Jews	9	7	—	− 7	− 5	—

TABLE 1 (Continued)

	Protestant	Catholic	Jewish	Protestant	Catholic	Jewish

Respect Beliefs of Others

F. "Compared with most people of your religious beliefs, would you say that most _____ are about the same, better, or not as good in respecting beliefs of others?"

	Percent Not as Good			Change Since 1952		
	Protestant	Catholic	Jewish	Protestant	Catholic	Jewish
Protestants	—	9	18	—	− 1	+ 10
Catholics	28	—	45	− 7	—	+ 10
Jews	11	5	—	− 5	− 5	—

Vote for a _____ President

G. "Would you vote for a _____ for President of the United States as for someone of your own religious faith?"

	Percent Yes			Change Since 1952		
	Protestant	Catholic	Jewish	Protestant	Catholic	Jewish
Protestant	—	94	92	—	+ 2	+ 2
Catholic	65	—	86	+ 23	—	+ 27
Jew	51	83	—	+ 20	+ 26	—

Marry a _____

H. "Would you just as soon have a member of your family marry a _____ as someone of your own religion?"

	Percent No			Change Since 1952		
	Protestant	Catholic	Jewish	Protestant	Catholic	Jewish
Protestant	—	46	80	—	− 9	+ 12
Catholic	53	—	85	− 10	—	+ 17
Jew	60	55	—	− 15	− 17	—

_____ Employers Discriminate

I. "Do you think most _____ employers would discriminate against you because of your religion or not?"

	Percent Expecting Discrimination			Change Since 1952		
	Protestant	Catholic	Jewish	Protestant	Catholic	Jewish
Protestant	—	6	26	—	− 2	− 1
Catholic	12	—	37	− 8	—	+ 6
Jew	11	8	—	− 7	− 6	—

Stick Together Too Much

J. "Do you think _____ stick together too much?"

	Percent Yes			Change Since 1952		
	Protestant	Catholic	Jewish	Protestant	Catholic	Jewish
Protestants	—	9	9	—	− 2	− 10
Catholics	28	—	47	− 12	—	+ 3
Jews	37	43	—	− 4	− 5	—

Getting Too Much Power

K. "Do you think _____ are getting too much power in the United States?"

	Percent Yes			Change Since 1952		
	Protestant	Catholic	Jewish	Protestant	Catholic	Jewish
Protestants	—	5	8	—	− 3	+ 3
Catholics	30	—	30	− 11	—	− 6
Jews	14	12	—	− 20	− 21	—

TABLE 1 (Continued)

	Protestant	Catholic	Jewish	Protestant	Catholic	Jewish

Give Intelligent Leadership

L. "Compared with most clergymen of your religious preference, would you say most_____clergymen are about the same, better, or not as good in giving intelligent leadership to their followers?"

	Percent Not as Good			Change Since 1952		
Protestant	—	5	0	—	− 1	− 1
Catholic	10	—	25	− 3	—	+ 17
Jew	3	2	—	0	0	—

Promoting Understanding

M. "Compared with most clergymen of your religious preference, would you say most_____clergymen are about the same, better, or not as good in promoting understanding between their group and others?"

	Percent Not as Good			Change Since 1952		
Protestant	—	7	4	—	0	+ 1
Catholic	24	—	31	− 6	—	+ 17
Jew	11	6	—	− 1	3	—

Cooperating for Common Good

N. "Compared with most clergymen of your religious preference, would you say most _____clergymen are about the same, better, or not as good in cooperating with leaders of other religions for the common civic good?"

	Percent Not as Good			Change Since 1952		
Protestant	—	4	0	—	+ 1	− 4
Catholic	19	—	25	− 5	—	+ 13
Jew	9	2	—	− 1	− 4	—

Setting Good Example

O. "Compared with most clergymen of your religious preference, would you say most_____clergymen are about the same, better, or not as good in setting a good personal example?"

	Percent Not as Good			Change Since 1952		
Protestant	—	4	0	—	− 2	− 1
Catholic	14	—	10	− 4	—	+ 5
Jew	6	3	—	− 2	− 1	—

Try To Influence

P. "Do you think_____try to influence the press too much in favor of their religion or not?

	Percent Yes			Change Since 1952		
Protestants	—	7	6	—	− 6	− 5
Catholics	25	—	43	− 5	—	+ 7
Jews	4	5	—	− 5	− 5	—

TABLE 1 (Continued)

Magazines Try To Be Fair	Q. "Do you think ——————magazines try to be fair to your religious beliefs or not?"					
	Percent No			Change Since 1952		
Protestant	—	12	2	—	—	−12
Catholic	24	—	29	−7	—	+12
Jew	12	13	—	−2	−2	—

Unpleasant Personal Experience	R. "Have you or your family ever had any unpleasant personal experience that might have made you dislike ————?"					
	Percent Yes			Change Since 1952		
Protestants	—	4	9	—	0	+2
Catholics	7	—	15	−2	—	+4
Jews	5	5	—	−3	−1	—

TABLE 2
CHANGES IN JEWISH AND CATHOLIC ATTITUDES
TOWARD EACH OTHER (1952–1965)
(+ percent = favorable change; − percent = unfavorable change)

Item	Percent Change in Catholics Toward Jews	Percent Change in Jews Toward Catholics
Prejudice against other	+ 7	− 15
Prejudice from other	+ 6	− 14
Interfere with our liberties	+ 1	− 6
Unfair in business	+ 8	+ 2
Dishonest in public office	+ 5	− 8
Don't respect our belief	− 5	− 10
Would vote for the other as President	+ 26	+ 27
Would not want intermarriage	+ 17	− 17
Employers would discriminate	+ 6	− 6
Stick together too much	+ 5	− 3
Getting too much power	+ 21	+ 6
Clergymen not intelligent	0	− 17
Clergymen don't promote understanding	+ 3	− 17
Clergymen don't promote civic cooperation	+ 4	− 13
Clergymen don't set good personal example	+ 1	− 5
Try to influence press	+ 5	− 7
Their magazines not fair	+ 2	− 12
Have had unpleasant experience with other that caused dislike of other	+ 1	− 4

TABLE 3
ANTI-CATHOLIC FEELING AMONG JEWISH GROUPS

Anti-Catholic Feeling Among Jewish Groups	Young	Middle	Old	Grammar School	High School	College
Catholics look down	44	29	13	33	41	48
Catholics interfere	25	17	10	6	13	25
Catholics don't respect faith of others	56	46	28	13	31	60
Catholics discriminate	51	36	44	33	25	44
Catholics stick together	61	33	58	46	45	47
Catholics after power	31	27	31	20	27	33
Clergy not intelligent	36	22	14	7	12	38
Clergy doesn't promote goodwill	36	29	28	20	15	43
Number of responses	(36)	(42)	(29)	(15)	(44)	(69)

TABLE 4
JEWISH ATTITUDES TOWARDS CATHOLICS BY BELIEF IN GOD AND CONGREGATIONAL AFFILIATION

Jewish Attitudes Toward Catholics	Believe in God, Belong to Congregation	Believe in God, Do Not Belong	Do Not Believe, Do Not Belong
Catholics look down on us	57	36	36
Catholics try to interfere	30	34	7
Catholics don't respect our beliefs	62	63	22
Catholics discriminate	50	29	29
Catholics stick together too much	57	37	43
Catholics are getting too much power	33	34	27
Clergy not intelligent	40	29	12
Clergy doesn't promote understanding	43	32	27
Number of responses	(40)	(38)	(41)

TABLE 5
PERCENT OF DESIGNATED ITEMS BY EASTERN
AND MIDDLE-WESTERN ETHNIC GROUPS

Item	Eastern [a]				Middle-Western [b]			
	Irish	German	Italian	Polish	Irish	German	Italian	Polish
Score high on general knowledge	15	8	5	1	14	8	8	2
Belong to Democratic Party	76	56	67	70	64	67	69	80
Consider themselves "very happy"	45	36	33	32	34	35	37	29
Score high on piety	28	16	10	13	44	37	22	21
Score high on religious extremism	23	20	26	35	15	22	19	39
Score high on racism	44	51	50	54	41	48	48	64
Score high on anti-Semitism	31	44	44	55	30	53	45	53
Score high on open-mindedness	53	42	43	47	49	47	35	39
Score low on anomie	66	52	41	49	61	54	59	40

[a] New England and Middle Atlantic.
[b] East North Central and West North Central. Other regions are excluded.

TABLE 6

PERCENT OF DESIGNATED ITEMS BY THOSE NOT GRADUATING FROM HIGH SCHOOL AND HIGH-SCHOOL GRADUATES, BY ETHNIC GROUPS

Item	Did Not Graduate from High School					High-School Graduate				
	Irish	German	Italian	French	Polish	Irish	German	Italian	French	Polish
Hold prestige jobs	5	4	2	1	5	30	25	18	22	21
Work as professionals or managers	5	5	0	4	5	46	37	32	18	24
Earn over $14,000 a year	12	12	10	14	13	28	24	26	16	23
Score high on general knowledge	4	1	1	1	0	22	14	12	11	6
Belong to Democratic Party	79	69	79	75	83	67	63	59	63	70
Consider themselves "very happy"	28	29	30	39	22	44	40	40	40	32
Score high on piety	5	4	2	1	5	36	33	15	35	15
Score high on religious extremism	27	31	29	36	44	15	14	20	17	25
Score high on racism	55	54	58	56	64	43	36	48	28	60
Score high on anti-Semitism	36	61	51	60	60	28	40	37	46	44
Score high on open-mindedness	52	42	38	37	39	52	50	45	45	47
Score low on anomie	45	41	41	39	38	69	57	53	61	50
Number of responses	(72)	(131)	(175)	(101)	(96)	(256)	(230)	(195)	(76)	(87)

TABLE 7
PERCENT OF DESIGNATED ITEMS BY GENERATION AND BY ETHNIC GROUPS

Item	First and Second Generation					Third or Later Generation				
	Irish	German	French	Italian	Polish	Irish	German	French	Italian	Polish
Hold prestige jobs	21	14	10	5	12	25	20	16	12	16
Work as professionals or managers	21	17	26	10	18	24	29	27	17	9
Earn over $14,000 a year	24	15	20	7	20	24	21	13	8	17
Score high on general knowledge	19	10	5	3	2	18	10	16	7	5
Belong to Democratic Party	69	64	70	74	77	71	66	51	72	76
Consider themselves "very happy"	30	36	34	49	27	45	37	43	37	24
Score high on piety	32	23	13	26	19	32	33	11	23	16
Score high on religious extremism	16	20	26	26	38	17	20	12	27	20
Score high on racism	53	55	53	45	51	43	41	54	35	67
Score high on anti-Semitism	35	55	46	53	53	28	44	35	52	53
Score high on open-mindedness	55	42	40	34	47	51	50	45	44	37
Score low on anomie	52	48	47	49	48	70	54	50	60	43
Number of responses	(76)	(109)	(294)	(70)	(111)	(225)	(216)	(62)	(79)	(58)

TABLE 8
DESIGNATED ITEMS BY ETHNIC GROUPS

"Taken all together, how would you say things are these days—would you say that you are *very happy, pretty happy,* or *not too happy?*"

A. Happiness (Percent)

Item	WASP	Irish	Polish	Italian	Jewish
Very	37	44	28	31	14
Pretty	47	38	59	52	55
Not too	16	18	13	17	31
Number of responses	(227)	(64)	(39)	(59)	(43)

B. Attitudes on Race (Percent)

Item	WASP	Irish	Polish	Italian	Jewish
Negro children should go to separate schools	64	20	38	17	30
Negroes should be on separate sections of streetcars and buses	22	5	21	14	8
Unfavorable to Negroes living in same block	41	25	46	36	30

C. Voting in 1960 Election (Percent)

Item	WASP	Irish	Polish	Italian	Jewish
Voting for Kennedy	43	76	82	88	57

TABLE 8 (Continued)

D. Attitudes on Courtship Practices
(Percent Rating Practice as "Acceptable for Male
When He Is Engaged")

Item	WASP	Irish	Polish	Italian	Jewish
Kissing	96	95	97	91	92
Petting	63	55	70	42	63
Intercourse	18	22	13	5	49

(Percent Rating Practice as "Acceptable for Female
When She Is Engaged")

Kissing	95	93	95	95	92
Petting	57	53	63	41	63
Intercourse	14	14	8	5	45

E. Attitudes Towards Drinking (Percent)

Item	WASP	Irish	Polish	Italian	Jewish
Abstainers	33	11	10	10	23
Twice a week	28	41	32	15	44
Neglect meals	14	17	17	6	25
Don't remember next day	14	12	11	4	17
Toss down fast	26	28	19	7	35
Makes socializing more enjoyable	36	64	74	45	38
Makes less self-conscious	19	27	18	11	14

TABLE 9
POLITICAL AFFILIATION BY FATHER'S ETHNIC BACKGROUND
(Percent for June 1961, College Graduates)

Political Affiliation	Protestant				Catholic				Jewish		Black
	English	Irish	German	Scandi- navian	Irish	German	Italian	Polish	German	Polish	
Democrat	25	28	21	22	41	37	37	48	36	49	80
GOP	48	45	56	49	30	35	38	24	21	14	—
Independent	24	22	25	25	26	23	31	26	40	34	17
New Left	1	2	2	2	2	1	1	0	1	1	1
Other	2	3	6	2	1	4	3	0	2	2	1
Weighted Number of responses	1,775	304	1,059	360	366	336	199	111	60	333	76

TABLE 10
PERCENT LIBERAL, IN RANK ORDER, FOR JUNE, 1961, COLLEGE GRADUATES

Rank Order by Religion and Ethnicity	Percent
Black	83
German Jew	82
Polish Jew	69
Catholic Pole	62
Catholic Italian	56
Catholic Irish	55
Protestant Irish	53
Protestant Scandinavian	51
Protestant English	49
Protestant German	45
Catholic German	44

TABLE 11
PERCENT OF JUNE, 1961, COLLEGE GRADUATES HIGH ON SUPPORT OF STUDENT MILITANCY

Rank Order by Religion and Ethnicity	Percent
German Jew	50
Polish Jew	45
Black	39
Protestant Scandinavian	33
Catholic Irish	29
Protestant Irish	28
Catholic Pole	28
Catholic Italian	24
Protestant English	23
Protestant German	21
Catholic German	20

TABLE 12
PERCENT OF JUNE, 1961, COLLEGE GRADUATES HIGH
ON FEDERAL AID TO COLLEGES

Rank Order by Religion and Ethnicity	*Percent*
Black	56
Polish Jew	41
Catholic Irish	32
German Jew	30
Catholic Pole	30
Catholic Italian	27
Protestant Scandinavian	26
Protestant English	22
Protestant German	20
Protestant Irish	18
Catholic German	17

TABLE 13
ARTISTIC AND READING HABITS OF JUNE, 1961,
COLLEGE GRADUATES

High on Art Scale		*High on Reading Scale*	
Rank Order by Religion and Ethnicity	*Percent*	*Rank Order by Religion and Ethnicity*	*Percent*
German Jew	39	German Jew	37
Polish Jew	31	Polish Jew	25
Protestant Irish	30	Protestant Irish	23
Black	27	Protestant Scandinavian	23
Protestant Scandinavian	24	Protestant English	23
Protestant English	21	Catholic Irish	23
Protestant German	19	Catholic Pole	22
Catholic Irish	19	Black	20
Catholic Italian	19	Catholic Italian	18
Catholic Pole	17	Protestant German	17
Catholic German	13	Catholic German	16

TABLE 14
CAREER CHOICES OF JUNE, 1961, COLLEGE GRADUATES
BY RELIGION AND ETHNICITY

Academic Career Choice		Private Business Corporation Career Choice	
Rank Order by Religion and Ethnicity	Percent	Rank Order by Religion and Ethnicity	Percent
Catholic Pole	23	Catholic Pole	41
German Jew	17	Catholic German	41
Protestant Scandinavian	17	Catholic Italian	36
Catholic Irish	16	Protestant English	30
Protestant Irish	15	Protestant German	30
Black	14	Polish Jew	30
Protestant English	13	German Jew	28
Polish Jew	11	Catholic Irish	22
Protestant German	11	Protestant Scandinavian	22
Catholic German	8	Protestant Irish	21
Catholic Italian	5	Black	9

TABLE 15
IMPORTANCE OF RELIGION AND ETHNICITY
(Percent)

Items	Irish	German	Polish	Italian
Belong to one or more religio-ethnic organizations	46	50	22	22
Closest friend Catholic	81	78	72	82
Feels most at home among coreligionists	34	17	37	32
Loyalty to religious group most important sign of good Catholic	45	42	68	62
Religion most important group membership	57	57	52	52
Spoke foreign language as child	0	27	68	50
Follows Old World customs now	19	16	55	43
Followed Old World customs as child	17	25	68	63
Number of responses	(47)	(39)	(51)	(40)

TABLE 16
ATTITUDES TOWARDS CHILD REARING
(Percent)

Items	Irish	German	Polish	Italian
Shouldn't doubt parents' ideas	22	30	46	48
Should not question thinking of parents	20	25	36	34
Parents should never look bad	40	61	60	65
Nothing worse than hearing criticism of mother	48	59	70	75
No excuse for upsetting confidence in parents	52	65	76	75

TABLE 17
ATTITUDES AMONG ETHNIC GROUPS
(Percent)

Attitudes	Irish	German	Polish	Italian
High on anomie scale	32	31	47	42
U.S. should help under-developed countries	85	77	73	80
Poverty results from lack of education and lack of opportunity	86	76	80	79
Government should spend so much on poverty	56	62	54	68
No objection to Negroes living on block	40	46	34	29
Negroes in congregation would be "fine"	28	41	13	22

TABLE 18
ATTITUDES AMONG ETHNIC GROUPS
REGARDING RELIGION AND HOLIDAYS
(Percent)

Attitudes	Irish	German	Polish	Italian
Family had special ways of celebrating religious holidays	76	79	92	80
Special foods	58	32	72	72
Church attendance	72	41	56	30
Special decorations	50	51	27	33
Special food at Christmas	93	76	86	78
Special food at Easter	73	69	84	73
Easter decorations	55	66	70	62

TABLE 19
ETHNICITY AND INVOLVEMENT
(Percent)

Involvement	Catholic					Protestant			Jewish
	Italian	Irish	German	Polish	French	English	German	Scandi-navian	
High on socializing scale	29	37	31	24	24	35	33	38	39
Belong to PTA	62	68	65	44	30	58	50	68	87
Belong to no organizations	62	57	63	66	83	56	53	40	45
Met new people	39	50	49	39	26	58	50	54	43
Number of responses	(300)	(244)	(159)	(86)	(118)	(343)	(239)	(51)	(176)

TABLE 20
ETHNICITY AND SELF-DESCRIPTION
(Percent)

Self-description	Catholic					Protestant			Jewish
	Italian	Irish	German	Polish	French	English	German	Scandi-navian	
Very sociable	34	24	17	19	11	21	25	10	21
Enjoying everything	30	36	34	24	20	24	24	26	24
Worry all the time	26	12	17	24	14	11	14	10	25

TABLE 21
ETHNIC BEHAVIOR BY SOCIAL CLASS
(Percent)

Ethnic Groups by Religion	Low (Duncan Occupational Prestige Scale [1–5])					High (Duncan Occupational Prestige Scale [6–10])				
	N	High on Socializing	Visit with Parents Every Week	Visit with In-laws Every Week	Visit with Siblings Every Week	N	High on Socializing	Visit with Parents Every Week	Visit with In-laws Every Week	Visit with Siblings Every Week
Catholic										
Italian	(178)	33	86	65	69	(76)	38	70	55	53
Irish	(121)	39	57	51	55	(108)	45	40	47	42
German	(99)	32	62	51	40	(50)	38	26	26	15
French	(71)	20	62	65	48	(25)	30	52	64	37
Polish	(52)	21	72	55	43	(19)	38	51	41	50
Protestant										
English	(140)	34	43	41	32	(150)	44	32	28	20
German	(99)	24	50	53	40	(95)	46	38	27	22
Scandinavian	(23)	22	47	30	26	(21)	59	27	32	17
Jewish	(49)	30	51	56	44	(113)	43	60	60	34

TABLE 22
INTERACTION WITH RELATIVES BY CLOSENESS
OF RESIDENCE OF ETHNIC GROUPS BY RELIGION

A. Interaction with Parents Who Live in . . .

Ethnic Group by Religion	Same Neighborhood	Same City, Different Neighborhood	Different City
Catholic:			
Italian	100	87	33
	(66)	(62)	(46)
Irish	100	70	18
	(22)	(45)	(69)
German	100	76	15
	(12)	(41)	(54)
French	95	77	26
	(22)	(22)	(31)
Polish	100	86	26
	(6)	(20)	(13)
Protestant:			
English	96	60	12
	(35)	(43)	(104)
German	100	74	21
	(16)	(36)	(81)
Scandinavian	100	87	5
	(4)	(8)	(19)
Jewish	?? 91	62	37
	(12)	(48)	(27)

B. Interaction with In-laws Who Live in . . .

Ethnic Group by Religion	Same Neighborhood	Same City, Different Neighborhood	Different City
Catholic:			
Italian	93	67	28
	(37)	(65)	(44)
Irish	90	61	16
	(20)	(53)	(47)
German	89	53	20
	(9)	(35)	(41)
French	95	60	35
	(20)	(25)	(23)

TABLE 22 (Continued)

B. Interaction with In-laws Who Live In . . .

Polish	77		71		0	
		(9)		(17)		(16) ?
Protestant:						
English	89		52		16	
		(19)		(43)		(91)
German	94		70		9	
		(16)		(29)		(56)
Scandinavian	100		83		13	
		(7) ?		(5)		(19)
Jewish	100		59		35	
		(11)		(16)		(25)

C. Interaction with Siblings Who Live in . . .

Ethnic Group by Religion	Same Neighborhood	Same City, Different Neighborhood	Different City
Catholic:			
Italian	94	62	26
	(89)?	(95)	(86)
Irish	95	60	19
	(36)	(88)	(96)
German	89	41	7
	(18)	(52)	(70)
French	79	46	20
	(24)	(26)	(52)
Polish	78	53	8
	(20)	(35)	(24)
Protestant:			
English	84	46	5
	(39)	(75)	(174)
German	81	47	13
	(27)	(60)	(112)
Scandinavian	62	49	12
	(5)	(10)	(31)
Jewish	100	43	7
	(19)	(67)	(71)

Bibliography

Abramson, Harold J. "The Ethnic Factor in American Catholicism: An Analysis of Inter-Ethnic Marriage and Religious Involvement." Unpublished Ph.D. dissertation, University of Chicago, 1969.

American Jewish Committee. *The Reacting Americans: An Interim Look at the White Ethnic Lower Middle Class.* New York: The American Jewish Committee, 1968.

Banfield, Edward C., and Wilson, James Q. *City Politics.* Cambridge, Mass.: Harvard University Press, 1963.

Bennis, Warren, and Slater, Philip E. *The Temporary Society.* New York: Harper & Row, 1968.

Bradburn, Norman M., Sudman, Seymour, and Gockel, Galen L. *Racial Integration in American Neighborhoods.* Chicago: Quadrangle Books, 1970.

Chesterton, Gilbert K. *The Napoleon of Notting Hill.* New York and London: J. Lane, 1914.

Cox, Harvey. *The Secular City.* New York: The Macmillan Co., 1965.

———. *Feast of Fools.* Cambridge, Mass.: Harvard University Press, 1969.

Cullinan, Elizabeth. *House of Gold.* Boston: Houghton Mifflin, 1970.

Danzig, David. "The Social Framework of Ethnic Conflict in America." Paper delivered at National Consultation on Ethnic America, Fordham University, June 20, 1968, sponsored by the American Jewish Committee.

Edwards, David L. *Religion and Change.* New York: Harper & Row, 1970.

Eisenstadt, S. N. *Essays on Comparative Social Change.* New York: Wiley, 1965.

Ferkiss, Victor. *Technological Man, the Myth and the Reality.* New York: George Braziller, 1969.

Fishman, Joshua A. (ed.) *Language Loyalty in the United States.* London and The Hague: Mouton, 1966.

Fitzpatrick, Joseph. "Intermarriage of Puerto Ricans in New York." *American Journal of Sociology* 71 (November 1966): 395–406.

Francis, E. K. "The Nature of the Ethnic Group." *American Journal of Sociology,* 52 (1945): 393.

Gans, Herbert. *The Urban Villagers.* Glencoe, Ill.: The Free Press, 1962.

Geertz, Clifford. *Islam Observed.* New Haven: Yale University Press, 1969.

Gilkey, Langdon. *Naming the Whirlwind.* Indianapolis: Bobbs-Merrill, 1969.

Gill, James. "Why We See It in Priests," *Medical Insight* (December 1969), 21–32.

Glazer, Nathan. "Ethnic Groups in America." Part of the symposium *Freedom and Control in Modern Society* by Monroe Berger, Theodore Abel, and Charles H. Page. New York: Van Nostrand, 1954.

———, and Moynihan, Daniel Patrick. *Beyond the Melting Pot.* 2nd ed. Cambridge, Mass.: MIT University Press, 1970.

Gordon, Milton. *Assimilation in American Life.* New York: Oxford University Press, 1964.

Greeley, Andrew M. "Some Aspects of Interaction between Members of an Upper Middle-Class Roman Catholic Parish and Their Non-Catholic Neighbors." Unpublished M.A. dissertation, University of Chicago, 1961.

———. *Religion in the Year 2000.* New York: Sheed and Ward, 1969.

———. "The Positive Contributions of Ethnic Groups in American Society." Paper presented at a meeting sponsored by The American Jewish Committee, May 1970.

Greeley, Andrew M. *The Denominational Society*. In preparation.
——, Marty, Martin, and Rosenberg, Stuart. *What Do We Belive?* New York: Meredith Press, 1967.
——, and Rossi, Peter H. *The Education of Catholic Americans*. Chicago: Aldine, 1966.
——, and Spaeth, Joe L. *Recent College Graduates*. New York: McGraw-Hill, 1970.
——, and Spaeth, Joe L. "Stratification, Poverty, and Social Conflict in American White Ethnic Groups." In *Stratification and Poverty*, edited by Seymour Martin Lipset and Michael Miller, forthcoming.
Hentoff, Nat. "Counterpolitics: The Decade Ahead." *Evergreen Review* (February 1969): 25.
Herberg, Will. *Protestant-Catholic-Jew*. New York: Doubleday, 1955.
Houtart, François. *Aspects sociologiques du catholicisme americain*. Paris: Les Editions Ouvrières, 1957.
Jencks, Christopher. "Private Schools for Black Children." *The New York Times Magazine* (November 3, 1968): 30.
Kennedy, Ruby Jo Reeves. "Single or Triple Melting Pot? Intermarriage Trends in New Haven." *American Journal of Sociology* (January 1944), 331–39.
Lerner, Michael. "Respectable Bigotry." *American Scholar* (August 1969).
Levine, Edwin M. *The Irish and Irish Politicians*. Notre Dame, Ind.: Notre Dame Press, 1966.
Levine, Irving M. "A Strategy for White Ethnic America." Paper delivered at Conference on the Problems of White Ethnic America. University of Pennsylvania, June 25, 1968, sponsored by The American Jewish Committee.
Lorenz, Konrad. *On Aggression*. Translated by M. Wilson. New York: Harcourt, Brace and World, 1966.
McDermott, John. "Laying on of Culture." *The Nation* (March 10, 1969).
Parenti, Michael. "Ethnic Politics and the Persistence of Ethnic Identification." *American Political Science Review* (September 1967).
Religion Reported by the Civilian Population of the United States: March, 1957. Series P-20, no. 79. Washington, D.C.: U.S. Government Printing Office, 1958.
Reports of the Immigration Commission: Abstracts of the Reports of the Immigration Commission. Vol. 1. Washington, D.C.: U.S. Government Printing Office, 1911.
Reports of the Immigration Commission: The Children of Immigrants in Schools. Vol. 1. Washington, D.C.: U.S. Government Printing Office, 1911.
Rosenthal, Erich. "Studies of Jewish Intermarriage in the United States." *American Jewish Year Book* 64 (1963).
Schaar, John. "Reflections on Authority." *New American Review* 8 (1970): 671.
Sklare, Marshall. "Intermarriage and the Jewish Future." *Commentary* (April 1964).
Stinchcombe, Arthur L. "Environment: The Cumulation of Events." *Harvard Educational Review* 39 (Summer 1969).
Stouffer, Samuel A., and others. *The American Soldier: Adjustment During Army Life*. Princeton, N.J.: Princeton University Press, 1949.
Suchman, Edward A. "Sociomedical Variation Among Ethnic Groups." *American Journal of Sociology* 70 (November 1964): 319.
Thomas, William I., and Znaniecki, Florjan. *The Polish Peasant in Europe and America*. Chicago: University of Chicago Press, 1918.

Weber, Max. "The Ethnic Group." In *Theories of Society*, edited by Talcott Parsons. Vol. 1. Glencoe, Ill.: The Free Press, 1961.

Whyte, William F. *Street Corner Society: Social Structure of an Italian Slum*. Chicago: University of Chicago Press, 1955.

Wilson, James Q. "Generational and Ethnic Differences Among Career Police Officers." *American Journal of Sociology* 69 (March 1964): 522–28.

Index

Abramson, Harold, 89–93, 169
acculturation, 24–25, 57–59, 169;
relationship to income levels, 32;
stages, 53
affluence, and ethnic differences, 103–104
Agenda for the Nation, 172
alienation, of white ethnics, 97, 153–65
American Jewish Committee, 173, 175–76
American Political Science Review, The, 14–15
American Scholar, The, 120
American Soldier, The, 188, 192
anomie, 188, 191
anti-Semitism, of ethnic groups, 66–73, 201, 202, 203
Armenians, 23, 24, 178; acculturation, 25; differences from other ethnic groups, 26
assimilation, 53–59, 106; types, 24–25

Banfield, Edward, 189
Baptists, 87
Bellah, Robert, 83
Bennis, Warren, 98, 184
birth control, 141
black militants, 60, 63, 157, 164
Black Panther Party, 131, 157
blacks, 17–18, 62, 64, 74, 75, 175;
acculturation, 25, 57; artistic and reading habits, 208; attitudes of ethnic groups towards, 155–57, 204, 210; career choices, 209; compared to Irish, 34–35; conflicts with Jews, 34; conflicts with Poles, 33–34, 170–71; differences from other ethnic groups, 26; education, 29; ethnic consciousness, 14, 17–18; income levels, 30, 31; and intellectuals, 124–25, 127, 129; liberal views, 207; and New York teachers' strike, 20–22; and politics, 14, 206; relations with Jews, 20–22, 34; and student militants, 207; in unions, 63–64
block busting, 155
"blue-collar problem," 182
Boston, Mass., 27, 28, 121, 156

Catholic Church, 63; ecumenism in, 141; Germans and, 142; Irish and, 141–45; "underground church," 144
Catholics, 62, 63, 73–80, 84–85, 105–106, 153; acculturation, 57; artistic and reading habits, 208; attitudes, 66–73, 195–200, 207; career choices, 209; conflicts with Jews, 171; and education, 208; ethnic behavior, 212–15; interethnic marriage among, 89–93; in Ireland, 42; and Jews, 179–81; and politics, 206; as superethnic group, 24
Center for Dispute Settlement, 172
Chicago, Ill., 49, 63, 121, 129, 131, 161, 173; ethnic conflicts in, 33–34; Polish community in, 47
Chicago, University of, 101, 121, 174
Chomsky, Noam, 125, 129
classical sociology, 184–91
Columbia University, 173
community, quest for, 100–101
community organizations, 173–74
conflict, 60; types, 64–65
consensus, 165
Consultation on Church Unity, 85
Coser, Lewis, 60–61
counterculture, 148
country clubs, 106–109
Cox, Harvey, 99–100
"cultural pluralism," 24, 25
"culture lag," 99

Daley, Richard, 18–19, 129
Danzig, David, 172–73
demagogues, 163–64, 171
Democratic party, and ethnic groups, 22, 62, 73, 79–80, 201–203, 206
Depression of 1929, 146, 153
Dillingham Commission, 28–32
discrimination: against blacks, 18–19; against white ethnics, 18–19; attitudes by religious groups on, 196
Dissent, 122
drugs, 145, 148
Duff, Edward Father, 57
Durkheim, Emile, 183

About the Author

The Reverend Andrew M. Greeley, Ph.D., is Director of the Center for Ethnic Pluralism of the National Opinion Research Center at the University of Chicago and Professor of Higher Education at the University of Illinois. He is Associate Editor of the *Review of Religious Research* and a member of the editorial board of *Sociological Analysis*. He served on the Planning Committee of the 1969 National Conference on Higher Education.

Father Greeley has written more than a dozen books on the sociology of religion and religious education, including *Religion and Career: A Study of College Graduates* (1963); *The Education of Catholic Americans* (with Peter H. Rossi, 1966); *The Catholic Experience: An Interpretation of the History of American Catholicism* (1967) and *What Do We Believe?* (with Martin E. Marty and Stuart E. Rosenberg, 1968). He also writes a syndicated column for the Catholic press.